SEVEN BIBLICAL DIRECTIONS FOR MANHOOD

GENE MASON

© 2025 Gene Mason
All rights reserved. No portion of this book may be reproduced, stored in a retrieval system, or transmitted in any form or by any means—electronic, mechanical, photocopy, recording, scanning, or other—except for brief quotations in critical reviews or articles, without the prior written permission of the publisher. Version 4.0

Cover image used under license from Shutterstock.com.

All Scripture quotations, unless otherwise indicated, are taken from the Holy Bible, New International Version®, NIV®. Copyright ©1973, 1978, 1984, 2011 by Biblica Inc.® Used by permission. All rights reserved worldwide.

ISBN 979-8-218-62832-1

Published in Atlanta, Georgia by Leadership Ministries, Inc.

FOR LEVI

> "WHO AM I? THAT'S THE REAL QUESTION, ISN'T IT? WHAT OTHER QUESTIONS ARE THERE?"

CONTENTS

Foreword 7

Then... You Walk Into the Volcano 9

A Man Works 31

A Man Loves 49

A Man Guards 65

A Man Fears 81

A Man Fathers 101

A Man Serves 127

A Man Walks 147

Walk Like a Man 167

Endnotes 177

SOCIETY EXPECTS
BOYS TO BECOME
MEN—GROW UP,
GO TO SCHOOL,
CHOOSE A CAREER,
BUILD THEIR LIVES
AND FAMILIES.
BUT MANY ARE NOT.

FOREWORD

In his bestselling book, *Good To Great,* Jim Collins defines a Level Five Leader as one who blends personal humility and professional will, prioritizing the organization's success over personal recognition. This is the type of leader I have observed in Gene Mason over the last five years. Gene has poured his life into the organization I founded in 1983.

Gene's book is *Walk Like A Man.* Throughout the scriptures the concept of walking with God is prevalent. It is the picture God uses to describe a man's life overall, his walk with the Lord. Paul writing to the Colossians tells them that he is *"... praying that they would walk in a manner worthy of the Lord, pleasing him in every way, bearing fruit in every good work and increasing in the knowledge of God" (Colossians 1:10).*

Here is what I have seen in Gene: He is a real man. He works like a man. He works tirelessly on important matters, strategic issues: Speaking, writing, editing, coaching, training, all aimed at helping spread the Gospel of our Lord Jesus Christ.

This results in changed lives. Men become more effective in their marriages, their families and their business lives.

Gene loves like a man. He and Keri love their three adopted children. He loves the men whom he serves in the fellowship. He goes the extra mile. Distinctive of Gene is that he loves the "hard to love" (I may be one of them). He *"guards his heart with all diligence for out of his heart come all the issues of life" (Proverbs 4:23).* He is a mature Christian leader. He worked for 35 years as a communications expert in large churches and marketplace companies. Over the last five years I have seen Gene be instrumental in our ability to successfully transition to a wider and global vision. Leadership teaching we created has been downloaded more than 650,000 times.

Gene shepherded the book, *Meet Me On Friday Morning.* He was a key player in getting it published. The strategy of Friday Morning Men's Fellowship is the *table...* a meeting of men shepherded by a trained leader, where lives are changed through intelligent discussion of the Scriptures. The men are in an environment which breaks down barriers. That is because there are no religious overlays or pretense. Gene has been instrumental in protecting these distinctives.

I do hope you enjoy *Walk Like A Man.* I have found it to be both enjoyable and educational. I plan to use this book as a resource for my own life and ministry.

Chris White
Founder, Leadership Ministries Inc.

THEN... YOU WALK INTO THE VOLCANO.

Joe's life had little meaning. He had a dead-end job in a dim office. The fluorescent tubes above his desk flickered to the point they literally sucked the life out him. He didn't keep himself well—tangled hair, sloppy clothes, worn out shoes. He was mildly humorous, but it was the kind of sarcastic, observational quips that one made because they had nothing of value to add to a conversation. You wouldn't pick Joe out on the street. You would pass right by him without a second glance. He was, in a word, unremarkable.

Earlier in life Joe had done things that were meaningful, even heroic, but that was years in the past. Today he had no family to speak of. He had accomplished nothing of merit. He knew no one. To make matters worse, a doctor told Joe he had a terminal disease, with just weeks to live. What terrible luck! His meaningless life would soon end, and nobody would notice. Joe seemed relieved that he wouldn't have to keep going. Disappointed for sure, but what did he have to live for anyway? So, an oddly horrifying plan by a wealthy businessman was intriguing to him, even well-received. After all, Joe Banks had nothing to lose.

The proposal went like this: Joe would experience week of high-life living—anything he could want he would have the money to buy. Then there would be a trip to an exotic, remote island, the journey itself beautiful and a grand adventure. At the center of the island was a volcano that erupted every 100 years, unless the gods that governed it were appeased by a human sacrifice. It had been 99 years, 11 months and some days since the last eruption, so disaster was imminent. The island was of great value to the wealthy man. He had to do something to appease the angry volcano gods so he could hang on to the island's riches. Joe would be paid to make the ultimate sacrifice. The rich man said it ended his proposal in a simple flat tone: "Then, you walk into the volcano."

A life ended. And, after all, Joe was about to die anyway. An offering made. The gods satisfied. Joe's life had meant very little. But his death would have great meaning. He would save an island and its people. All it would take is a short walk. A love story then unfolds during Joe's last great adventure, and the tale builds to its volcanic climax. A destructive eruption is imminent! All the while we wonder, will Joe muster the courage and willpower necessary to walk to his fiery death?

It's not a true story, of course. It's the somewhat morose plot of the romantic comedy *Joe Versus The Volcano*. Joe was played by Tom Hanks, opposite his frequent love interest in

1990s films, Meg Ryan. In the movie, Joe Banks is already an adult, but he's not yet a man. The story shows how he moves from being aimless and alone to having a purpose and a relationship. That journey to manhood is something that all men approach, but some never go through. It's an old movie, long forgotten by most. But today's world is filled with Joe Banks-type males, wandering aimlessly, seeking and searching, and deeply in need of a walk into something meaningful.

While I was watching the movie, I kept wondering, "Why in the world would Joe do this?" As the plot goes along the audience starts to like Joe. He has great qualities. He's kind, funny, romantic. What is he trying to prove by walking into the volcano? Joe is trying to find himself, to see what he is all about. At one point Joe says, "Who am I? That's the real question, isn't it? Who—who am I? Who are you? What other questions are there?"

By the end of the movie, Joe has figured it out. There's only one problem though—he no longer wants to walk into the volcano. When he finally understands what it means to be a man, his life has once again become too valuable to offer it to the volcano gods on a tiny island nobody has ever heard of.

I resonate a little with Joe Banks. There's been a portion of my life when I was rather aimless. I didn't know what I wanted for a career, so I also didn't know what I wanted to study in school. I liked to escape of movies and books because they took me to far off places with no decision-making required.

I kept thinking, maybe at some point a volcano will come along—some grand thing that I can stand on for purpose and meaning. But it never did.

I still remember a guy from high school named Michael. From the first time I met him, he said, "I want to be a doctor." He was very focused on it. He knew exactly where he wanted to go to college, what specialty he wanted to study. He went to medical school in the same city where I lived, so I would see him at church on occasion. "Michael, are you a doctor yet?" I would ask. "Not yet, but I'm working on it," he would answer. This went on for years. I'd pass him in the hall or see him at the Kroger. "Doctor?" I'd ask. "Not yet."

Eventually I moved away. Then some years later on Facebook I saw his profile. Dr. Michael. Biologist. Surgeon. Married. Two kids. He hadn't wasted a minute. I was jealous. I wish I had that clear path for myself in life and work. I had spent some time wandering about without forward motion and purpose. Dr. Michael had, with intent, walked right into his volcano. He knew what he wanted from life and went down that path, no reservations.

The man game
There's a ton of extended adolescence in our society. Males who, for one reason or another, never reach point where they graduate from boys to men. Another movie that comes to mind is *Failure to Launch* starring Matthew McConaughey. In the film, McConaughey plays 35-year-old Tripp, who still lives with his parents. He has a job, but spends his nights going out on

surface dates, playing video games or drinking beer. Whenever a relationship begins to get serious, Tripp stages an awkward encounter and breaks up. He refuses to leave the nest. His purpose is on hold, and he never launches into self-sufficient adulthood. In the movie, his mom and dad hire a consultant, a woman, to grow close to him and lure him out of the house.

Despite the comedy of *Failure to Launch,* this is not a fictional phenomenon. As of 2021, about 35% of all US adult men, ages 25-34, still live at home.[1] The percentage is even higher for men in Europe—in Greece it's 80% of young men still at home! Men are also increasingly isolated, remaining single through more of life. About four in ten adult men—38% between the ages of 25-54—are single. This is up sharply from 30 years ago, when the percentage was 29%.[2] Society expects boys to become men—to grow up physically, go to school, choose a career path, move out on their own, and begin building their lives and families. But many are not.

A stereotypical "good man"

In society, there's fast-fading picture of a traditional "good man". You might identify with parts of the stereotype. He was born to a two-parent home. As a boy, he enjoyed playing outdoors, made friends, took up sports. His mom doted on him, made sure he tucked his shirt in and washed behind his ears. His dad played catch, took him fishing or hunting, instilled discipline. His family ate meals regularly at the kitchen table. Mom and dad insisted his hair didn't touch his collar. They'd take him to church every Sunday even though he protested.

One Sunday he listened intently to the sermon and decided to turn his life over to Jesus. As a teenager he gravitated toward football, friends, girls. He was smart, funny, relaxed. He lost his virginity his senior year in high school, but no baby resulted, so he chalked it up to experience and determined to be more serious with relationships going forward. He did well in school and chose a college that mom and dad could afford on his partial scholarship. He loved university life, waited tables to save up money, studied hard, and graduated.

After college he found a good entry-level position at a firm downtown. A young woman he met at the university happens to work nearby. They dated for a number of years, then got married. Four years later they have two kids with a third on the way. He put his savings into a first house and a better car for his wife. His mom and dad are proud grandparents and still stop by regularly to visit. The young father has steady work, a solid marriage, a growing family, and a spiritual foundation. He volunteers at church and is a regular in his small group. He's far from perfect, but he is faithful, and honest, loving, and a leader.

This is one picture of the typical "good guy". The desired elements in this lifestyle for the adult man is healthy, long-term relationships, stability at home, a growing career, and an active spiritual life. But most of those elements aren't typical anymore. Fewer than half of all men—46%—grew up in a home with two married heterosexual parents in their first marriage.[3] Today about 41% of all males are born to couples outside of wedlock—in 1960 it was just 5%. The number of men growing up in traditional home environments, then going on to form their own traditional homes, is slim. A third of kids today live with an unmarried parent (just 9% in 1960) and a rising number of kids are living with no parent at all—instead a grandparent, relative or foster family. About 70% of all married men and women with kids have two-income households. With both parents out of the house daily, iPhones and YouTube have become substitutes for childcare. Without traditional moms and dads, we're not raising well-adjusted kids. And we've lost a generation or more of traditional men.

Full stop

I started out in a traditional family that came to an abrupt halt. My parents divorced when I was 16. My dad had an affair with his secretary, and then married her. It was a rocky relationship all around. They divorced a year later. Dad kept up with my mom and supported her after the marriage, setting her up in a house and paying her bills. After a while they started talking again and amazingly were remarried 11 years later. Time actually does heal some wounds. They remained married until mom's death in 2022 from frontotemporal dementia. They both did the traditional parenting when I was a kid—until they didn't. After they got back together my dad never spoke of the divorce. My mother occasionally referred to it as dad's "oopsie."

Like so many other families, the role of man laid out for me was incomplete. I had a fuzzy picture of fatherhood in my teen years. Then I saw dad brazenly betray mom. I still loved him because he was my dad, though mom was heartbroken. Dad was around, but kept his thoughts to himself and faded from influence in my life. Later as a young adult, I didn't have clear idea of where I was going, or what I wanted to accomplish. Even being deeply involved in church didn't really provide me mentoring or discipleship. I knew a lot about God, but very little about being a godly man. As a kid I wanted to please my dad and looked up to him. As a young adult, having seen some of his failures, I didn't want to be anything like him.

I made many mistakes, broke relationships, hurt friends. I constantly put my naïve view of the world, life, and my own interests ahead of everything else. The idea of godly manhood is something I wouldn't zero in on until much later. Why did God make me a man, and what kind of man do I want to be? I was in my 40s before I honestly started asking these kinds of questions of myself.

I wanted to be accepted in God's eyes, pleasing to my wife, strong for my kids. How do I work out each of these areas? Honestly, I'm still working it out. Once I began to study manhood in the Scriptures, I realized that there is much I could learn about being a godly man. The Bible does give a strong, clear picture of what a real man looks like.

What is a man?

If we believe that God is the Creator of the universe, it follows we must also believe those areas of life that He has clearly defined for us. The Creator defines His Creation. Not only do we have our physical bodies to examine for evidence, but we are given God's Word, the Bible, as a help to understanding

DON'T LOSE THE MARVEL OF MANHOOD! GOD MADE YOU A MAN BECAUSE IT IS THE BEST EXPRESSION OF YOU THAT CAN EXIST.

our nature. God created man and woman separately and uniquely, with specific roles. Genesis 1:27 reminds us, *"So God created mankind in his own image, in the image of God he created them; male and female he created them."* That last phrase, *"male and female he created them,"* is a statement of specific intent.

Intentionally created
Sex and gender are not fluid. They are intentional. The word "created" in Genesis indicates man was not an evolution, a malleable amalgam of cells to be defined more fully later on. Man was a new, precise, distinct work. Recent cultural thought degrades God's gender intent at conception to a hiccup of happenstance, like a mole or hair color. "You came out of the womb a man, but that is something you can always change later if it suits you." This line of reasoning leads a male on a quest for what might make him happy or satisfied, instead of to where he will actually find satisfaction—growing as God's intentional creation.

Man is God's highest-order creature, the last great act of His creation. Man was created in God's image, meaning he possesses characteristics of his Creator. The Bible says, *"He created them male and female and blessed them. And he named them 'Mankind' when they were created" (Genesis 5:2).* Male and female were not designed to be "separate but equal", but rather, "specific and unique".

God made man for a reason, and gave him capabilities and capacities that differed from women because God also gave man his own set of duties. Don't make the mistake of thinking you just happen to be a man.

The Bible, along with thousands of years of the culture of mankind, outlines man's responsibilities in life. Among those are providing fathering, food, shelter and protection for wife and mother, and children. To do this, man is created generally with greater strength, musculature and endurance to do these things well.

Further, the Bible gives detailed instruction to people—especially men—on how to act and live in the image of their Creator. Men are to lead the home, spiritually and personally, and are held accountable by God for the stewardship of their family. The Apostle Paul repeats God's command succinctly in his letter to the Corinthian church: *"Be watchful, stand firm in the faith, act like men, be strong" (1 Corinthians 16:13).*

Do you read Paul's command to *"act like men"* and know how to apply what he is teaching? He wrote it assuming there would be little question to it. Actor John Wayne once said, "I want to play a real man in all my films, and I define manhood simply: men should be tough, fair, and courageous, never petty, never looking for a fight, but never backing down from one either." That's good old cowboy real-man talk! But is that what it means to be a man?

God-given responsibility

We must understand the God-given function and responsibilities of men. Then we must teach our sons to grow up and to *"act like men".* We must take on the God-ordained tasks of man and to do those to the very best of our ability. The call of godly manhood is to put aside our own wants and desires in life and act like men, through the pursuit of Christ and obedience to God's Word. It's the picture our Creator envisioned for His great handiwork. Don't lose the marvel of manhood! If God made you as a man, He did so because it is the best expression of you that can possibly exist.

After God creates man on Day 6, He takes a break. Genesis 2:1 says, *"By the seventh day God had finished the work he had been doing; so on the seventh day he rested from all his work."* These verses aren't showing God as exhausted from creating the world and man. God doesn't come in from the yard drenched in sweat and needing a glass of water. No, creation took no more effort by God than the snap of a finger. It was a beautiful act of creation that culminated in man breathing in for the first time and opening his eyes. For God it was the final brush stroke on His incredible masterpiece. And so, God stepped back on Day 7 to admire His creation, as an Artist does when He completes His work. Man was a picture in God's image, good and worthy and filled with purpose.

Culture shifts
Two fundamental shifts have occurred in culture with respect to men. First, the equality movement that began some 50 years ago. This is not the "equal rights" movement, where men and woman are treated equally in society, with the right to vote, to work, to education, etc. Those are good things! No, the equality movement sought to erase the differences

between men and women, in order to make them "equal" in all respects. "Anything a man can do, a woman can also do."

This is true in some ways, but in other ways it simply denies the differences in the sexes. There are some things a man can do that a woman cannot (provide sperm). There are some things a woman can do that a man cannot (birth a child, breast feed). Activist Gloria Steinem said, "A gender-equal society would be one where the word 'gender' does not exist: where everyone can be themselves." But that's not true. A genderless society would rob men and women of the wonderful and miraculous differences between the sexes, squelching the unique strengths of each. The world needs men and women, and for men and women to understand their strengths as men and women.

In addition to physical differences, there are areas of mental development that vary. A woman is generally a better nurturer, with greater emotional intelligence. A man tends to focus on one task or area of expertise instead of multitasking. These differences shouldn't be erased, but rather celebrated, and honed for the advantage of humanity, and within the individual family. Instead of accepting the idea of men and women as equal, we should focus on what makes each sex a unique, wonderful, God-designed work.

A second cultural shift is the more recent gender movement, which tries to separate sex and gender and redefine them as choices in life, versus distinct and physically defined at conception. For the mammals *homo sapiens,* the science of sex

WE ARE NO LONGER SYSTEMATICALLY TEACHING BOYS WHAT IT MEANS TO BE A MAN. THEY LACK THE KNOWLEDGE OF MANHOOD, AS WELL AS ANY CONCEPT OF THE RESPONSIBILITIES OF A MAN.

is clear down to the chromosomes. Biologist Walther Fleming discovered chromosomes in the late 1800s, and named these complex cells "chromatin" because of their unusually strong sustained properties. That is, they do not change, despite cell division and growth. The chromosomal package of DNA is exactly as God designed, male or female, from conception to birth through growth and life and then in death.[4] A man is a man, a woman is a woman, for their entire existence.

Gender activists have sought to separate these facets, with sex being a person's physical attributes—male or female based on their various body parts. A modern definition of gender is a person's social role—their mannerisms and behaviors associated with men or women. But this again denies reality. Gender is deeper than dress, makeup or mannerisms. Just because someone acts like a man or woman doesn't mean they are of that gender.

Today we live in an odd time, where some encourage men and women to "change genders" if they feel in any way uncomfortable with their minds and bodies. We latch on to momentary gender dysphoria that most children feel at some point in their early curious childhood ("I wonder what it's like to be a boy/girl?") and convince them to "transition" instead of embrace the amazing person they are in God's image. We would not allow a child to get a tattoo because of the permanent nature of the art, but for some reason we may allow some doctors to permanently alter a child's physiology and mutilate their bodies attaching the macabre title "gender affirming care", often without the knowledge or consent of a parent. Our society will eventually realize the great cost of this terrible evil.

These are not just personal or religious beliefs. They are facts established by God and true for millennia. Doesn't it seem particularly odd that instead of trying to understand what it means to be a man or woman, so many in our culture are content to throw out their birthright and pursue a counterfeit version of the other sex?

The decline of manhood
As a result of these movements, we face a cultural decline in manhood. We attach words to masculinity like "toxic" and "patriarchic". Some go as far as to consider anything related to man as "triggering"—offensive or psychologically damaging. Most of the traditional avenues for development into manhood—from Boy Scouts to the YMCA, to men's boarding schools, to school sports teams—have become "unisex". We argue about the gender of bathrooms. Department stores sell female swimsuits with pouches for male genitalia. A recent article in *Business Insider* detailed 259 LGBTQ characters in children's cartoons.[5]

Abnormal views on manhood are treated as normal and normal views are treated as repressive or insane. We are no longer systematically teaching boys what it means to be a man. Boys lack the knowledge of manhood, as well as any concept of the responsibilities of a man. Adult males do not know how to live and act as men. Paul's statement to *"act like men"* today might as well be "build a spaceship". We do not know where or how to begin.

In looking at the responsibilities assigned to man by God as written in the Bible, we'll quickly discover what manhood means. What is man supposed to do? It's not to twiddle around on earth for eighty years and then sit on a cloud, playing a harp in the sun, for all eternity. No! God has a role, a *walk*, for man. And like Joe and the volcano, the walk itself will define us, and grow us, and make us into men. It is time to walk like a man!

Knights and chivalry
In the Middle Ages, noblemen were the land owners. They built homes with strong walls to protect from enemies, which eventually became castles. To watch over those who lived under their protection they had knights, a brave and strong warrior class. Even today, knighthood is a title conferred to someone for their service to a monarch or the Christian church, typically in a military capacity. From its origins in the twelfth century, the title of knight recognized the most noble and elite class of warrior. The word *knight* comes from an Old English word meaning *servant*. Associated with knighthood was an informal code of conduct known as *chivalry*.[6]

Author Tonke Dragt wrote, "Not only must a knight be able to use weapons and prove himself knowledgeable in many fields, but above all he must prove that he is chivalrous and honest, brave and true. He must be knightly in every respect." Chivalry defined the perfect courtly Christian warrior—brave, honorable, courteous, good mannered and with a readiness to help the weak. Always championing the right and the good against injustice and evil. In a word, a gentleman.

THE WORLD DOESN'T NEED MORE THUGS, OR STUDS, OR WOKE APOLOGISTS. THE WORLD NEEDS REAL MEN. KNIGHTLY MEN, FULL OF CHIVALRY, SERVICE, HONOR.

A knight was to always be generous, upright, distinguished and trustworthy. While some early knights did indeed pillage and loot when fighting for their noblemen leaders, most knights were of religious orders, which included vows of poverty and chastity. The Knights Templar order fought during the Crusades in the 1100s. The Knights Hospitaller were formed in 1023 to protect the poor and the sick.

Can you recall any man who is *knight-worthy* that you know today? A man who, upon first meeting them, immediately displays trustworthiness? A man who by their very demeanor, words and actions, conveys the thought, *I am safe with this person?* Do you know a man would defend you if necessary, lives with honor, is upright, distinguished, brave, true?

Just as the knight's armor has gone obsolete, so too in our age has the concept of chivalry. As we've tinkered with the roles of the sexes, we've lost somewhat the idea of a knightly man, who holds a woman in high esteem and looks after her safety and security. This is much more than opening the car door for her. It's a deep and abiding admiration for women that causes a man to rise to the noblest expression of his own character. Men today have a lesser respect for feminine qualities. The concepts of chivalry, while somewhat romanced in literature, haven't found a home in modern culture.

We are losing the ability to know how to treat one another honorably and courteously within the traditional gender roles. Also lacking is the principle that a man's life is lived in service to noble pursuits, and to aid the less fortunate. The knights of the Middle Ages were trusted men, defenders of their lord's lands and people. Today's man plays video games into his 40s and lives in his parents' basement. No wonder many women ask, "Where have all the good men gone?"

I believe chivalry should make a comeback. We should embrace the concept and act like gentlemen. We should pursue virtue and treat women with tender care. You may think these ideas are obvious, but they're not. If they were, we would be quite a different society today. Instead of building up men and teaching them God-honoring ways, we're abandoning the concept of manhood entirely! It is to the detriment of our culture and future.

The world needs more men. My neighborhood needs more men. My wife and kids need a man. The world doesn't need more men who are thugs, or studs, or woke apologists. The world needs *real men.* More *knightly men,* full of chivalry, service, honor. Men of character. Men committed to learn and pursue their God-given purposes. Men who positively impact those around them and focus on others in a way that makes the world a better place in which to live.

The seven walks of man

In trying to understand how to be a gentleman, a real man, I took a journey through Scripture. In God's Word I found seven areas of instruction to men. Together they are helping me to form a picture of God's desire and role for man and manhood. I long to live out these principles on a daily basis. I want to *walk like a man,* just as Adam did in the Garden of Eden. To

A DEEP AND ABIDING ADMIRATION FOR WOMEN CAUSES A MAN TO RISE TO THE NOBLEST EXPRESSION OF HIS OWN CHARACTER.

stroll along with God Creator in the cool of the day, talking about why He made me and fulfilling those tasks that He has given me.

Want to do the same? Then walk along with me for a while, and consider how God made man, and what he is designed to do. Then perhaps at the end if I've made a compelling argument, you might join me in this noble, if somewhat difficult, pursuit. I'm going to try to do my best to *man up*, to sacrifice my wants for the greater good, to focus on godly principles, and to muster up the courage and fortitude to walk into that volcano...

Find your volcano:

- *What God-given responsibilities are you uniquely suited to accomplish, because you are a man?*

- *What facets of manhood are a great challenge to you? What is ahead of you that feels like Joe Versus the Volcano?*

- *Have you ever struggled with manhood? Have you delayed growing in independence from your parents, and choosing a life direction and path that fosters your development as a man?*

A MAN WORKS

*"I have two doctors,
my left leg and my right."*
—G.M. Trevelyan

Jhaqueil Reagan was 18 years old, had no money and no job, and was homeless. He'd been sleeping on a friend's sofa. It was March of 2013. The weather that day in Indianapolis was bitter cold, with ice and snow covering the ground. Jhaqueil was energized. He had a promising job interview, but had no way to travel the ten miles between the couch and the business. It wasn't a slam dunk, and it was for minimum wage, but that was more than Jhaqueil had in his pocket—so he thought it worth the effort.

That's why you would have seen Jhaqueil Reagan walking along the road that day. Determined, he decided to bundle up as best he could, and walk the ten miles to the interview, legs trudging through the piles of slush the plows had pushed off to the side of the road. "That's the kind of story your parents used to tell, my parents used to tell, up hill both ways in the snow," Jhaqueil said. The wind was biting, and the passing cars threw sleet into his face, but Jhaqueil soldiered on. About halfway there, he wasn't quite sure of his destination, so he stopped at a gas station to ask someone for directions. That's when he had a chance encounter with Art Bouvier, a local restaurant owner.

"I'm thinking to myself, here's a kid walking ten miles in the slush for the hope of a job at minimum wage," Bouvier said. Impressed with his tenacity, Art offered Jhaqueil a job on the spot—at double the minimum wage. Jhaqueil was delighted and smiled wide. The story soon made the local news and went viral. Jhaqueil was on his way.

Bouvier connected him with a local landlord who saw the story and rented him an apartment. "It really has changed quick," Jhaqueil said. "I went from sleeping on a couch to sleeping in my own house, you know, my own apartment." He still didn't have a car, but friends at work started giving him rides. The transit authority gave him a free bus pass. A local cell phone provider got him a phone. Jhaqueil was a model employee. The locals stopped by his work to patronize the restaurant and participate in his success.

As the story grew, the restaurant got busy and hired extra staff to keep up with demand. People kept calling the restaurant to offer donations—so much so that Jhaqueil started a foundation to help other disadvantaged people find work. "My cashiers have turned into receptionists," Bouvier the owner commented, pointing to a list of people who called and wanted to help. He also has a box full of slips with even more names and numbers. "Each slip is an individual contact of a person with a name and a number and they want to give financially," Bouvier said. Jhaqueil also gave a portion to the other restaurant employees, who had been working extra to cope with the demand.[7]

Work changed Jhaqueil's life. He had money in his pocket, a place to live, a group of fellow employees that supported him, a boss that cared, steady activity, a community that rallied to his aid, and a charity through which he could say "thank you" by giving back. It's an incredible story, that all started with a teenager's walk to work.

Made to work
Every able-bodied man should work. It's not a suggestion or preference. The Bible shows it is, in part, what man was made for. In Genesis 2, God had finished the work of creation. *"Then the Lord God took the man and placed him in the Garden of Eden to cultivate and keep it" (Genesis 2:15).* God gave man a job to do in the Garden of Eden. Notice this is before man ate the forbidden fruit, before sin entered creation, and before man was thrown out of the Garden. From the very beginning, as a part of God's perfect design, work was given to man.

Regularly scheduled maintenance
God made earth in a manner which required work to keep it up, and man has that assignment. Ever wonder why the world needs a maintenance guy? God did not have to create earth in this way—He could have made it completely self-sustaining.

But He structured the world in a way that the hand of man was needed. Because work is a part of God's perfect design, man can find joy, purpose and fulfillment in his work.

Why did God give man work? Chiefly to glorify Himself. It pleased God to see His finest creation filled with purpose and duty and tasks. These energize man's mind and body. His hands and legs, strength and balance and stamina, all engaged. Man's senses, taking in everything around him, sights and sounds and smells and touches. Man's thoughts, planning and thinking and determining. Every facet of this creature, man, that God had made, was coming into his fullness as he did the work that God had laid out for him. And all this was pleasing to the God Who had formed him to see to the Garden's needs.

Out of work
In 1953, 98% of US men between the ages of 25 and 54 had a job.[8] This high percentage of working men was also enjoying an unprecedented high standard of living—some 35-40% were unionized and able to support their entire family on their income alone, which became known as a "family wage." But this high standard has collapsed. Today, 28% of men of prime working age are not working.[9] Though the official unemployment rate among males is about 3.5%, this is a misleading indicator. It does not count men who have given up looking for work, or live solely on benefits. Let's also not forget to count the two million nonworking men in the US that are in prison—that's five times the number of men in prison in the 1970s.

EVER WONDER WHY
THE WORLD NEEDS
A MAINTENANCE GUY?
GOD MADE EARTH
IN A MANNER WHICH
REQUIRED WORK
TO KEEP UP. MAN HAS
THAT ASSIGNMENT.

Ecclesiastes 3:12-13 mentions work as a gift God gave to man. Solomon wrote, *"I perceived that there is nothing better for them than to be joyful and to do good as long as they live; also that everyone should eat and drink and take pleasure in all his toil—this is God's gift to man."* Many men consider work a burden versus a gift, and for this reason they lack a sense of personal accomplishment. Nonworking men are generally less educated, less likely to be fathers, less likely to seriously date or marry. Nonworking men not only don't work, the majority of them also don't fulfill other roles of manhood in society.

Aimless men also waste an enormous amount of time. Nonworking adult males spend an average of seven hours every day in personal leisure—relaxing, playing games, watching TV, scrolling the Internet. Government payments, fewer trade classes offered in schools, an attitude among males that they are unappreciated or taken for granted, and old-fashioned laziness, has resulted in fewer adult men engaging in purposeful work. The great dreams of American society have morphed along with them. "The pursuit of happiness" became the lesser "pretty good for all" to "my life's not so great—but I live through that celebrity influencer who flies private."

The joy is gone
Man's joyful work was lost when he sinned and was kicked out of the Garden of Eden. His holy work in the garden instead becomes toil. God commanded, *"By the sweat of your brow you will eat your food..."* (Genesis 3:17-19). Throughout the Old Testament, work is, in part, a punishment. It's arduous.

The Garden was perfect, but now there are thorns and hard soil and pests and rot and unbearable heat and cold. Much of the toil of work remains today as we live in a fallen, sinful world.

When man is restored to fellowship with God through Christ, his God-centered work returned. Paul writes in Ephesians 2:10, *"For we are his workmanship, created in Christ Jesus for good works, which God prepared beforehand, that we should walk in them."* Now man in Christ has a new assignment—good works on the earth that God has prepared for him to do. The Bible contains additional instructions about man and his work:

- *"But if any man does not provide for his relatives, and especially for members of his household, he has denied the faith and is worse than an unbeliever"* (1 Timothy 5:8). Man is to be a provider for his household through his work.

- *"Whatever you do, work heartily, as for the Lord and not for men..."* (Colossians 3:23). A man's effort in work is a reflection of his relationship with God.

- *"But let each one test his own work, and then his reason to boast will be in himself alone and not in his neighbor. For each will have to bear his own load"* (Galatians 6:4-5). A man's work is his personal responsibility.

- *"So God blessed the seventh day and made it holy, because on it God rested from all his work that he had done in* creation" (Genesis 2:3). Man is made in the image of God, and his work is a reflection of God's own effort in creation that He Himself refers to as "work".

- "Whoever is slothful will not roast his game, but the diligent man will get precious wealth" (Proverbs 12:27). The Bible draws a distinction between a man who works diligently to produce what he needs, and the lazy person who does not provide for himself. Men aren't lazy.

- "There is nothing better for a person than that he should eat and drink and find enjoyment in his toil. This also, I saw, is from the hand of God..." (Ecclesiastes 2:24). God desires man to enjoy his work, because it was given to him by God to do.

Yes, you should work

We define work as a regular activity requiring mental and physical effort in order to achieve a purpose. Do you have a job, duty, function or assignment that is your work? According to the Bible, an able-bodied man should work diligently, in the most basic sense to provide for himself and his family. He should use his skills and abilities to accomplish the purposes of God, to fulfill his personal responsibilities. He should enjoy his throughput and accomplishments.

Work for man, according to Scripture, is not optional. It is a spiritual necessity which has, in our fallen world, also become a practical necessity. How, then, might we grow in manhood through work?

Understand work as a spiritual discipline

The desire to do something meaningful is built into our consciousness as a reflection of our Creator. Regard work as an act of obedience to God. A man doesn't work just to earn a paycheck. Rather, he first works because God designed him for work. It is in his work that a man also fulfills the spiritual function for which God made him. Take up the mandate in Colossians 3:23 and give your best effort in work: *"Whatever you do, work at it with all your heart, as working for the Lord, not for human masters."*

Work is not just a spiritual discipline, it's a ministry opportunity. Think about the opening a job provides to connect to people, serve others, share faith, pray for those in need, and fulfill God's purposes. Work provides occasion to the use your talents and skills for God's glory. Consider your work skills and experience and how these could be utilized, spiritually. A man at work is fulfilling one of the purposes for which God created him. Remember Jesus' instruction in John 6:27, *"Do not work for the food that perishes, but for the food that endures to eternal life, which the Son of Man will give to you."*

1 Corinthians 15:58 instructs men, *"Therefore, my beloved brothers, be steadfast, immovable, always abounding in the work of the Lord, knowing that in the Lord your labor is not in vain."* The Apostle Paul is connecting work to his relationship with God. The picture here is of plentiful, abundant labor in the life of the man. This strengthens the man in character and gives him spiritual purpose. Facets of what we do daily in the office, or job site, or business is *"of the Lord"*.

INSTEAD OF FLOATING
FROM JOB TO JOB,
A MAN CAN CHOOSE
A PATH THAT
ALLOWS HIM TO
GROW IN SKILL
AND LEADERSHIP,
AND MAINTAIN
A STABLE HOUSEHOLD.

Choose a career

Today the average man changes jobs every 4.1 years. About half the total US workforce changes jobs every five years.[10] Though "moving up" at work is desired, don't discount the benefits of sticking with the same field of work over an extended period. A long-term career in a specific industry include higher salaries over time, performance bonuses, pension plans, healthcare benefits and more paid time off. Long-term employees may also have access to additional training and development programs.[11] Having a career plan promotes financial stability and security. You may still change jobs from time to time, but understanding what you bring to the table in your job. Think seriously about where you want to be professionally in five years, ten years. This helps you make wiser choices for your work.

When it comes to work, the Bible is clear—get to it! Remember 2 Thessalonians 3:10: *"For even when we were with you, we would give you this command: If anyone is not willing to work, let him not eat."* The lesson in this verse is not to hunker down and hustle. Instead, it is to engage in work with a goal in mind. You might work at a job you don't love to earn a paycheck and provide for your household, or you might work at a job you deeply enjoy in order to advance a business, product, idea or invention. You might work at a nonprofit to improve the human condition. You may work in ministry to evangelize and disciple your neighbor.

In Bible times, the vast majority of men were farmers. For 10,000 years, societies were agrarian, only becoming industrialized in the last 250 years. A man's time was spent each day growing food (or fishing or hunting) for himself and his family. Centuries of this lifestyle solidified man's role as a provider. Scripture affirms this role, encouraging man to work the land diligently. Proverbs 12:11 says, *"Whoever works his land will have plenty of bread, but he who follows worthless pursuits lacks sense."*

Today, a career provides a sense of diligence for the working man. Instead of floating from job to job, a man chooses a work path that allows him to continue in a familiar direction, grow in skill and leadership, and maintain stability for his household. A career gives a regular paycheck. It can be appealing intellectually. It often comes with a sense of identity—he's a doctor, a builder, a teacher, a driver, a salesman, a lawyer. 1 Thessalonians 4:11 admonishes men *"to aspire to live quietly, and to mind your own affairs, and to work with your hands..."*

Settle down

Family responsibility is a great motivator that enjoins your work to personal growth. Unmarried men are less likely to work than those who are married, healthy and have children. For a married man, work becomes a facet of his family life, versus a preeminent focus. In the economy of God, a career provides stability, and a family provides companionship and emotional security. Many men conflate a career with life purpose—"I was made to be a (fill in the work-blank)." They might derive their entire identity from their work. The Bible instead tells us that our work is a facet of our God-given mission. Proverbs 16:3 reminds us, *"Commit your work to the Lord, and your plans will be established."*

Instead of a constant push to advance, the Bible also teaches a man to direct energy to grow in His relationship with God, and to invest in the people around him. Psalm 90:17 tells us *"Let the favor of the Lord our God be upon us, and establish the work of our hands upon us; yes, establish the work of our hands!"*

Unfortunately today many men look to celebrities, sports figures or successful CEOs as examples to follow. A far better standard to look to for manhood is what we might call the "family man". He is married with one or more children, has a career and home. Settling down in life and work adds a facet to a man's character—*devotion*. A devoted man derives great value from his family and work relationships. Work is the engine that allows him to provide for and minister to those around him. A devoted man lives for his people, not for his work.

Don't live for work

My dad was a workaholic. He was a sales manager for an insurance company. He built out an office in our basement and spent his days there on the phone and doing paperwork. He had a full-time secretary named Ruth that had a desk next to dad's. There were shelves and files, stacked with forms and brochures and books of tables and charts and actuarial figures. Ruth would leave at 5:00, and at night after dinner, dad would settle down in his recliner in our den, where there were piles of papers and files laid out on the floor surrounding him. He'd kick up his feet and keep on working while the rest of the family watched TV or did homework.

Occasionally dad traveled. Any trips we took as a family had an element of his work involved. At one point he decided to buy an airplane so he could go farther for work. He went to Panama City Florida to flight school to get his pilot's license. We stayed on the beach in a condo for a month having a blast on a super-long vacation. But we seldom saw dad, who had his books open on the dining table studying about winds and flight plans and navigation.

A few years later his insurance company had their annual convention at Walt Disney World. The whole family went. Dad was present at his meetings and gatherings and talked with other insurance people, while mom took my brother and I to the theme parks. We saw dad at night for dinner, but otherwise he was working. We'd tell dad about riding the monorail, meeting Micky Mouse, getting wet on the river ride. He missed all of it.

For dad, the solution to any issue in life, family, marriage, was to work more. This did two things—it took him out of the conversation about a problem, and it gave him an excuse for his absence. He was just too busy. If you ask me today to describe my dad as I was growing up, I would say, "He was always working."

I've had a tendency to be a workaholic as long as I can remember. Obviously I took that cue from my father. For the better part of three decades, I threw myself into work as much as possible. Sometimes I worked 80 or more hours a week. I had a full-time job and then several side-hustles. When my future wife and I began counseling before marriage, she expressed concern about my constant work. I said, "Sure, I'll slow down once we are married." But I didn't. Starting in year three of my marriage, I worked two jobs constantly for the next fifteen years.

The work overload ended badly. I had a health scare at age 49. That's also when I found out I had diabetes. I was literally working myself to death. Something had to change. I took a new job, and started working less, giving more time to my wife and family. At the time I did it because I was forced to. I wouldn't be alive if I didn't change. But later, I began to think through exactly how I had become so lopsided.

I realized that I didn't have a good understanding of God's purpose and design for work. I didn't work because God designed me for it, or choose a career and settle down for a spiritual purpose. The emotional escape and intellectual pleasure work had become for me made it an addiction. Just as not working is an unhealthy view of work for a man, overworking is equally sinful.

An accurate view

Very few people in my circle over the years had a clear and helpful view of work. Even people who would tell me to "slow down, get some rest, spend time with your family," in the next sentence would say, "Can you add this to your

A HEALTHY RELATIONSHIP WITH WORK IS SOMETHING YOU HAVE TO UNDERSTAND AND PRIORITIZE. NOBODY ELSE WILL DO IT FOR YOU.

plate?" Get in balance—as long as it doesn't affect what you're working on for me. If you're going to have a good relationship with work, it's going to be something you have to understand and prioritize. Nobody else will do it for you.

You might conclude the pandemic caused a big shift away from unhealthy work habits. But as of 2021, 52% of men were experiencing a sense of burnout at work—up 9% from pre-COVID numbers.[12] And it turns out that the 80-hour week I worked for years was child's play. The top 6% of earners in the US work as many as 90 to 120 hours a week. There is no 40-hour workweek for ambitious executives. They leave the house at 7:00 a.m. and get home at 9:00 p.m.—many of them seven days a week.[13] They might even brag about their work ethic, but it isn't anything to brag about. These people—almost all men—are so engrossed in their work they have no real relationships or commitments outside of it.

I believe a healthy work ethic is to understand what God wants from our work. He doesn't want us to love our job. He wants us to love and serve Him through our job. God wants us to choose a career to embrace stability, and to settle down as "family men" to grow in emotional security and personal devotion. He wants us to use our work to serve Him and the people in our lives. Work provides for the household, but it also helps a man grow in godly character, as he does what God designed him to do. *"I perceived that there is nothing better for them than to be joyful and to do good as long as they live; also that everyone should eat and drink and take pleasure in all his toil—this is God's gift to man"* Ecclesiastes 3:12-13.

The walk of work:

- *Write out a list of your talents and abilities that you engage and apply at work. Next to each of these, write one or two ways these could be used to minister to others.*

- *Pray for God to provide "good works for you to do" in advance (Ephesians 2:10). Ask God to help you glorify Him through your physical and mental efforts.*

- *Consider volunteering outside of your job/vocation for ministry work, through your local church or another charity or mission.*

- *Are you consulting God about your life and career choices, and is that direction one established by Him?*

A MAN LOVES

> *"Pursue some path,*
> *however narrow and crooked,*
> *in which you can walk*
> *with love and reverence."*
> —Henry David Thoreau

"I'm Gonna Be (500 Miles)" is a classic rock tune by The Proclaimers. It's a song about the lengths a man would go for love. The chorus says: "But I would walk five hundred miles, and I would walk five hundred more, just to be the man who walked a thousand miles to fall down at your door." It's catchy, but honestly nobody would really walk 1,000 miles for love. Or would they?

8,000 miles for love
Joseph Hilaire Pierre René Belloc (1870 – 1953) was a Catholic writer and historian. He was born in France, but grew up in England and was a member of the British Parliament. During his life he was also an orator, sailor, artist, satirist, soldier and naturalist. He wrote poetry and whimsical tales, and was a

master of the English language. He also drew masterful pencil sketches. Belloc was brilliant, thoughtful, and at heart, a romantic.

In 1890, before he made a name for himself, Belloc met Elodie Hogan, a beautiful American woman visiting England. He was immediately taken. From a few brief encounters, he became determined to seek her hand in marriage, even as Elodie returned home to San Francisco, California. Joseph began writing Elodie love letters, hoping to capture her heart, but to no avail. Her replies were friendly but distant. Joseph decided if he was to have any chance to win Elodie, he would have to travel to plead his love in person.

Joseph was only 20 years old and had little money. In 1891, he sold everything he had and purchased a steamship ticket to New York. When he arrived in the States, he began his journey by train to see Elodie in California. He only made it as far as Philadelphia when his money ran out. Joseph was an athletic man who had hiked extensively in Europe. So, he began to walk the 2,870 miles from Philadelphia to San Francisco. He earned money along the way by reciting poetry or drawing sketches of the owners of homes in which he would stay for a night. Sometimes he would do farm labor for a day. He literally worked and walked his way to California.

After three months, Joseph reached San Francisco, and Elodie was happy to see him. But Elodie's mother intervened, seeing no future for his daughter with the destitute Joseph Belloc, no matter how much he professed his love. Elodie's mother insisted her daughter join a convent, which she did. Elodie was off-limits to Joseph. After a visit of just a few days, a deflated Joseph began the long walk back to New York. He took far longer on the journey than he had spent in person with Elodie. A biographer later wrote of Belloc's walk, comparing the fruitless thousands-of-miles trek to Napoleon's winter retreat from Moscow. Dejected, Joseph steamed back to England, where he threw himself into activity to assuage his broken heart.

Joseph served in the French military to retain his dual citizenship. Then he entered Oxford University, where he excelled in debate and earned a degree. Having secured financing as a lecturer and educator, Joseph received word from America that Elodie had left the convent. In March of 1896, he again voyaged to the United States. He was now an educated man with a job waiting for him at Oxford, and hopeful that Elodie might reconsider marriage. For the third time, he traversed North America on foot, taking two months to travel to San Francisco. Through rain, snow, dirt paths, hills and mountains, rivers and streams, patiently and intently, Joseph walked. When he arrived, he found Elodie was gravely ill. Overwhelmed that they might be denied one another by death, and exhausted from the journey, Joseph collapsed. Just as the song said, "But I would walk five hundred miles, and I would walk five hundred more, just to be the man who walked a thousand miles to fall down at your door."

Elodie saw the anguish of Joseph's reaction, and understood that his love for her was extraordinary. Over the next few weeks, Elodie recovered, and after six years of courtship, Joseph Belloc and Elodie were married in California. They went on to move to the United Kingdom, where Joseph taught, and Elodie bore five children. They remained entirely devoted to one another until Elodie's untimely death in 1914 from cancer. Joseph lived another 40 years after her death, but never remarried. He had walked over 8,000 miles to secure his one true love, and held Elodie's memory close, wearing mourning clothes for the remainder of his life.[14]

Love is a fickle word

Joseph Hilaire Pierre René Belloc lived a classic love story. When you hear that Joseph loved Elodie, you know he meant it. Joseph loved Elodie enough to walk across the continental US three times to win her heart. The word love for him was deeply held, sacrificial, heart-filled, romantic, in many ways overwhelming. Joseph would never use the word love flippantly or casually. It held far too great a value in his life.

To claim that a man loves, we have to dig beyond the fickle word love to see what the Bible demands of us. Our English language limits love severely. We love our parents. We love our children. We love our wives. But we also love ice cream. We love football. We love a funny Facebook post. We use the same word to describe deep, lifelong relationships, and to complement what we had for a snack, or the color of a new jacket. The Bible has multiple words for love—three Hebrew words in the Old Testament and at least four Greek words in the New Testament. These languages give us a much deeper understanding of love, including facets like fidelity, mercy,

WE LOVE OUR KIDS.

WE LOVE OUR WIVES.

BUT WE ALSO

LOVE ICE CREAM.

WE LOVE FOOTBALL.

WE LOVE A FUNNY

FACEBOOK POST.

grace, forgiveness, faithfulness, salvation, romance, sacrifice, kindness, friendship, emotions, and more. All these aspects of character convey a richness and depth to the true meaning of what it is to love.

The Bible takes time to define the rich and deep concept of love in Paul's letter to the Corinthians: *"Love is patient, love is kind. It does not envy, it does not boast, it is not proud. It does not dishonor others, it is not self-seeking, it is not easily angered, it keeps no record of wrongs. Love does not delight in evil but rejoices with the truth. It always protects, always trusts, always hopes, always perseveres. Love never fails" (1 Corinthians 13:4-8).* Notice how many action words are associated with love in these verses. Clearly love is not simply an emotion, but the activities associated in response to that closely-held feeling.

The loving man

The Bible instructs all Christ-followers to love. It also gives specific instructions on love to men. God defines love as a deep affection or attachment that causes man to act with trust, compassion, romance or sacrifice. Love is an emotion that causes man to do something meaningful. If it's a feeling devoid of action, it's not love. That's why ice cream, football, and Facebook don't pass the love test—they're mere affectations.

Also worth noting is that when the Bible instructs man on love, it's generally not about sex. We do see a wonderful romance and sexual intimacy in the context of marriage demonstrated in the Song of Solomon. There we read of two people committed to one another, loving one another as individuals, speaking of each other's physical traits and of their character. Their physical relationship becomes the culmination of all the other expressions of love and companionship in their lives. Then the Apostle Paul gives us instruction on marriage in his letter to the Corinthians.

Man was not created primarily to be a lover—sex is a gift of God to be enjoyed in the context of marriage. When Christ says, *"Love your neighbor as yourself,"* He's obviously not talking about physical love, but of a godly affection that provokes a man to action on behalf of the other. The love of a man towards others, as described in the Bible, is demonstrated in four ways. It is the combination of these that illustrate God's call for men to love wholeheartedly.

A man loves with his life
God instructs men to love all people. God gives men specific commands on how to love. John 15:13 says, *"Greater love has no man than this, that someone lay down his life for his friends."* John is illustrating that a man's godly love is *sacrificial*, putting the interests of the other person above his own. This is a difficult teaching. If a man should be willing to give his life for another, then certainly lesser sacrifices—his own wants, position and possessions—take a back seat to godly love's mandate.

Paul expands on this in his epistle, writing, *"Do you not know that your bodies are temples of the Holy Spirit, who is in you,*

A MAN SHOWS SACRIFICIAL LOVE BY SETTING ASIDE SOMETHING HE MIGHT WANT IN FAVOR OF SOMETHING THAT ANOTHER PERSON NEEDS.

whom you have received from God? You are not your own..." (1 Corinthians 6:19). Man was not created for himself, his own desires or pleasure. He was created as a vessel to carry out God's commands. We are to lead selfless lives, and one way in which this is demonstrated is the degree to which we prioritize loving others more than ourselves.

Does John 15 just allude to Jesus' sacrifice of His life out of love for us, or is the Bible teaching here that we should also be willing to actually give our lives for others? The answer is two chapters back in John 13:15-17. Jesus said, *"For I have given you an example, that you also should do just as I have done to you."* What Jesus is teaching is that we have no right to avoid doing those things that Christ Himself was willing to do for others. John 15 punctuates the ultimate act of love.

In the ultimate sense, a man should be willing to love by giving his life. In a practical sense, he loves by setting aside his life's ambitions out of love for others. In marriage, a man often defers to his wife's needs. As a father, he looks after the needs of his children. In leadership, he may prioritize his peers and reports at work. A man shows sacrificial love by setting aside something he might want in favor of something that another person needs, because of his connection to and affection for them. A man *loves* when that emotion causes him to act sacrificially.

A man loves his wife

The modern stance for marriage is that it is a "partnership". That is, we enter as equals and have equal responsibility in all areas. But this is not at all the teaching of Scripture. For married men, the Bible teaches, *"Husbands, love your wives, just as Christ loved the church and gave himself up for her" (Ephesians 5:25).* Again, we read the language of sacrifice attached to a man's love.

Though a man is told to sacrificially love his wife, the wife is given a different command—to respect her husband. This does not mean a wife does not love her husband, but rather the husband prioritizes love and the wife prioritizes respect. Remember, man and women are separate, distinct creations. They have different body parts, different mindsets, and God gives them different instructions in various facets of life and relationships.

Marriage as a biblical concept is a sacred, holy act. We hear the term "Christ-centered marriage" in church. The idea is that when we marry, we do it as God intended and for God's glory. At the core it is an act of worship before God. Few people today marry for this reason. The divorce rate has fallen—not because fewer people are getting divorced, but because fewer are getting married. Many couples are content to just cohabitate as equals. And if it some point it doesn't work out, well, they had separate checking accounts the whole time. The spiritual flaw in this is a couple that puts their own quest for happiness ahead of God's desire for holiness—a marriage is a relationship *set apart* for God's purposes.

A real man loves his wife sacrificially. That means he is going to give up his desire to win, or be right, or have all that he wants, when it comes to he and his wife. The husband can really only be head of the home if the other members of the household—the wife especially—trust in his leadership. If the wife doesn't believe the husband has her best interest at heart, she's not going to give up control of the house, or her heart. Looking back at Ephesians 5 we also notice an additional challenge for men—our instructions aren't conditional. If our wife does not love us, or respect us, as we desire, that does not negate our responsibility as a man and as a husband.

When I look at my marriage, I can honestly say the majority of problems we've had along the way are because I didn't love my wife in the way Christ commanded. I treated marriage as a partnership instead of a sacred, holy union in which I had specific, God-given commands to follow. Many times, I have loved myself more—what I wanted to do, what I wanted to buy, how I wanted to spend my time, my dreams, my wants, my desires. Putting myself ahead of my wife in life is not loving her. It's loving me.

Had my wife not given me respect through her deference in areas where I wasn't living up to God's standard, we wouldn't be married today. When I read *"love your wife as Christ loved the church and gave Himself up for her,"* I find it a deeply challenging teaching that is hard to live out. This does not come naturally. I have to think about it, each and every time.

A man loves his enemies

During His teaching through the Sermon on the Mount, Jesus gives interesting instruction on love. He says, *"You *have heard that it was said, 'Love your neighbor and hate your enemy.' But I tell you, love your enemies and pray for those who persecute you. If you love those who love you, what reward will you get? Are not even the tax collectors doing that? And if you greet only your own people, what are you doing more than others? Do not even pagans do that? Be perfect, therefore, as your heavenly Father is perfect." (Matthew 5:43-44).*

Now we see another key facet of biblical love coming to light. Love is not only sacrificial, but *humble*, putting others' interests before our own, even those with whom we disagree or don't like. It's easy to love people who love us back, but real love, the kind that God expects of a man, is to love people who are not lovely. Jesus goes on to say that loving people who don't love you, who even hate you, is perfect love.

Most men if asked, "Name some people who are your enemies," would probably say they don't have any. But a cursory inspection of social media would seem to indicate otherwise. Someone doesn't have to point a gun at you to qualify as an enemy. Look at the way we treat people of other political persuasions. Or those who root for another football team. Or those who pull out a cigarette and start smoking in the next restaurant booth. Love your enemies? Well, okay Jesus, I can do that. But if Jesus had said, "Love those you disagree with. In fact, especially love those you disagree with," we might react differently. Some men wave to their neighbors next door, then later jump on their iPhones and flame everyone on X who dares utter a word of opinion that differs from their own. We create enemies instead of developing friendships. This is not God's way of love for a man.

A man loves his friends

The pop singer Whitney Houston had a hit with her 1985 song "Greatest Love of All". You might remember Whitney singing in her soaring voice: "Learning to love yourself is the greatest love of all." It was a beautiful song, but it's spiritually inaccurate. Self-love isn't great love. It's certainly not the kind of love that Jesus wants us to have.

The Bible tells Christians to love each other. Jesus taught, *"I give you a new commandment: love one another. As I have loved you, so you also should love one another. This is how all will know that you are my disciples, if you have love for one another" (John 13:34-35).* While men should love sacrificially, they should also love *selflessly*.

It's easy to be selfish in our culture. We're bombarded by media and ideas that compel us to seek our own self-interest. The ancient Roman philosopher Seneca wrote, "No man can live happily who regards himself alone, who turns everything to his own advantage." The Bible reminds us that men who look to themselves at every opportunity are essentially unloving. God may not call you to die for someone else. But He unquestionably calls you to take an interest in them. Jesus' words as recorded by the Apostle John reveal that people around us will know whether or not we follow Him by how we treat one another. *"This is how all will know..."*

JESUS MADE HIS SACRIFICE OUT OF LOVE FOR MAN. IT FOLLOWS THAT IF MEN ARE TO REFLECT CHRIST, OUR LOVE OF OTHERS MUST ALSO BE SACRIFICIAL.

My son Levi is my youngest child, and he has two older sisters. He adores them, but he's all boy. The way he shows interest and affection is wanting to jump on the trampoline or play video games, or take one of them down with a wrestling move in the living room. The girls would rather listen to Taylor Swift or shop for makeup on Amazon. This is a hard love to teach Levi—selfless love for your closest companions. Knowing how to be gentle versus rambunctious. Teaching him gentle ways to show affection, and also teaching his sisters that when he yells, "Come to the trampoline right now!" it's his way of being affectionate. Selfless love is putting the needs of others first, giving your best to them and wanting God's best for them because you love them.

A complete picture of love
The challenge for men when it comes to love as God commands, is that it is entirely outward-focused. A man is to love all those around him—wife, family, friends, enemies—selflessly and sacrificially. A man's love for others is to always be greater than his love for himself. The call is not to the fickle love we apply to ice cream or football. It's the 8,000-mile walk of love that Joseph Hilaire Pierre René Belloc did in pursuit Elodie. Love is, in fact, a pursuit, and not a momentary reaction. Love is an emotion that causes us to act.

For men, God's commands and expectations regarding love echo His own. Christ Himself laid down His life for us. It was a sacrifice He undertook willingly, and out of love for mankind that His Father had created. It follows if men are to reflect Christ, then our love toward others must also be sacrificial.

We show and prove our love through our willingness to forgo our own desires and preferences in deference to those we love, and even those we do not. In that love, we may be called upon to make an ultimate sacrifice. That is, as God demonstrates for us, the nature of love.

The walk of love:

- *Is there a preference or desire you have for yourself today that you can set aside out of love for someone else in your sphere of influence?*

- *Pray especially for those in your life who are not lovely, your adversaries and even enemies. Ask God to open up ways for you to show them love and meaningfully influence them toward Christ.*

- *Consider actions you can take this week to show love to your wife. Concentrate on small, daily acts of love versus grand gestures. Is there a preference she has that you can meet, a chore you can complete without her asking, or an opportunity for quality time with her that you can arrange (even if it's just 20 minutes)?*

- *What are you teaching your children, your sons and daughters, about love? Are you teaching your sons to love sacrificially and selflessly? Are you teaching your daughters what to expect from a man who is truly loving?*

A MAN GUARDS

*"Know when to walk away.
And know when to run."*
—Kenny Rogers

The sun is just a hint of light on the horizon, yet to rise, when 22-year-old Private First Class Jackson walks in the door for his shift. He changes methodically into his Army Dress Blues. His uniform is not just clean and sharp. It is perfect. Not a spec of lint. Every golden button or buckle is polished to a flawless shine. Not a hint of dust on his shoes, which radiate a mirror sheen, as does the brim of his hat. He is careful to avoid a fold or wrinkle as he slips on his jacket and straightens his belt. His medals and decorations are precisely aligned and pinned to his lapel, each one level and equidistant from the next.

He checks his M-14 rifle and attached bayonet to ensure every part is in place. Both his weapon and uniform will be inspected closely. If any item, any single element of Jackson's dress, his person, his rifle, do not meet the standard of perfection, then he will not walk today. Any flaw, however slight, brings dishonor to him and to his duty. But Jackson would not dream of letting down the Relief Commander, or the Sergeant of the Guard. He checks himself one last time in the mirror, turns, and readies himself for the walk. In moments he will report for duty.

The Third US Infantry Regiment is also known as "The Old Guard". They're among the most elite soldiers in the US Army, and they have a sacred duty. They guard the Tomb of the Unknown Soldier at Arlington National Cemetery. They've been guarding the Tomb 24 hours a day, 365 days a year, since 1937. The remains of three unknown soldiers are buried there—one from World War I, one from World War II, and one from the Korean War. The Tomb remembers all soldiers who died in the line of duty, and whose remains never came home from combat, or were not identified.[15]

The guards, also called Sentinels, walk the Tomb day and night. They do not wear rank insignia while walking, as they do not want to risk bearing a rank that could be greater than the those in the Tomb they are guarding. The walk itself has meaning. The guard walks 21 steps from one side to the other. The walk is 63 feet from end to end, so each step is precisely three feet. He turns 90 degrees and pauses for exactly 21 seconds, another 90 degrees and another 21 seconds, then walks 21 steps back. These motions and timings are to signify the 21-gun salute, the highest military honor. The walk is never interrupted. The Sentinels have kept watch at the Tomb through blizzards, hurricanes and scorching heat. Every hour, on the hour, the guard is changed through an elaborate ceremony.

Each move and step of the Sentinels is carefully rehearsed. The standard is perfection. Every sentinel must exhibit an incredible degree of flawlessness. Why? Sgt. First Class Dontae Walker comments, "We're not here for ourselves." The walk is to honor the dead. Trainees spend three hours a day walking in front of the tomb. Every step must be exacting. Every time. Even after being approved for guard duty, they continue to practice and hone their skills for months before earning the coveted and rare Tomb of the Unknown Soldier Guard Identification Badge.[16]

The creed of the Sentinels states, in part, "My dedication to this sacred duty is total and whole-hearted, and in the responsibility bestowed on me never will I falter. And with dignity and perseverance my standard will remain perfection. Through the years of diligence and praise and the discomfort of the elements I will walk my tour in humble reverence to the best of my ability…"

Something of value

Guard is from an old French word *garder*, which means "to keep watch over". We watch over things we want to protect, or keep from damage or harm. We guard that which we value. The Tomb of the Unknown Soldier points to our deep reverence for lives given in sacrifice. Go to a museum and you'll see dozens of guards walking the halls and standing near those works of high value. We place guards in jewelry stores and banks and at Buckingham Palace and around Air Force One. In recent years we've placed officers in schools to protect the children. When you see a guard near something it's indicative that there is something of tremendous worth that needs to be protected.

When the Bible tells us to guard something, we should take note of the fact that God considers it of great value. That is why when Scripture tells us *"Above all else, guard your heart, for everything you do flows from it"* (Proverbs 4:23), it causes us to look to what God values, and how we might protect it. God doesn't tell us to guard our valuables, our homes, our bank accounts, or even our wives and families. The one thing we must guard, above all else, is the heart.

The heart of man
The Bible's idea of the heart isn't the physical muscle we know. In Bible times, men did not know the medical function of the heart—to pump blood in order to oxygenate the body. It wasn't until 129 AD that the Greek scientist Galen discovered pulmonary circulation. In 1578, William Harvey determined the heart pumped blood through the body. What we did know in ancient times is that each person had a heartbeat, and if it ceased, that person would die. We understood that the heart is what drives a man.

The heart in Scripture represents the core of a man's being— all of his thoughts, emotions, motivations, intellect and desires. The heart drives where we choose to focus our lives. When 1 Samuel 13:14 recalls that David was *"a man after God's own heart"*, it's speaking of a man whose mind and body were in sync with where God wanted him to go and what God wanted him to do.

THE HEART IN THE BIBLE REPRESENTS MAN'S CORE—
ALL HIS THOUGHTS, EMOTIONS, MOTIVES, INTELLECT, DESIRES. THE HEART DRIVES WHERE WE FOCUS OUR LIVES.

Why guard the heart? The Bible also tells us that our hearts by nature are treacherous and evil. Jeremiah 17:9 says, *"The heart is deceitful above all things and beyond cure. Who can understand it?"* Sin has affected us at the deepest level. If the heart is open, exposed, rotted, then the entire man is decaying. The Bible's concept of the heart representing who a man really is continues to this day.

Sometimes we might use a phrase like, "Follow your heart". This is self-centered and wrong. What God wants us for us to follow after Him, so that He might transform our heart from the inside out. As Psalm 51:10 teaches, *"Create in me a clean heart, O God, and renew a right spirit within me."*

The heart takes priority
A few years ago I was in a meeting at work and didn't feel well. I had a sandwich for lunch and thought, maybe food poisoning? My coworkers said I looked pale. I considered driving over to the doc-in-a-box. After some coaxing, I ended up at the emergency room.

That's where I had a heart attack. I admit I was scared, but the doctors rushed in and calmed my nerves. If you're going to have a heart attack, take it from me, the best place to have one is in the emergency room. They have all the tools and medicines and processes and personnel to deal with it on the spot. I saw a well-oiled machine of professionals solve a medical crisis. Walk into a hospital and say, "I have chest pain," and see the doctors and nurses spring into action. The heart takes priority.

My heart attack was terribly inconvenient. I had a pile of tasks to do that day. I had some family commitments for the afternoon. Emails to go out. Projects to complete. Suddenly, though, laying on the gurney in the emergency room with tubes in both arms and doctors leaning over me, my heart—the physical one—took priority. It wasn't functioning correctly, and until it was, all other considerations were out the window. And so it is with the spiritual heart, the core of a man. If it's not beating properly then the whole of the man is under attack.

After the initial shock of that day, the heart attack passed. I was alone for a while in the CICU before my wife arrived. They put in a temporary pump to help my heart until I could have surgery. I was hooked up to a dozen machines that beeped in the background. I laid there with my eyes closed and felt my heartbeat. I thought, "What if it stops again?" I became aware of each beat, the muffled thump that kept me alive all these years. I hadn't thought about it before, but now it filled my thoughts entirely. I hadn't guarded my heart.

I had triple-bypass surgery the next morning, and another week in the hospital recovering. Then I had to start living differently. I had to start guarding my heart against further damage. I changed my eating habits. Lost some weight. Started moving about more. Before the heart attack and surgery I rarely took even a Tylenol. Now I had a little plastic container with ten pills a day to swallow. God commands man to guard his heart. This means to have a keen awareness of what is coming into your spiritual heart and mind, and the choices and actions that result from it. When you think about your physical heart, and the central role it plays in life itself, then the role of man's spiritual heart is easy to understand. How can we guard our spiritual heart? How can we ensure everything that flows from our heart makes us a stronger, better, godly man?

Keep your diet healthy

A man guards his heart with a keen sense of what goes into it. The average person has between 12,000 and 60,000 thoughts per day. Of these, 95% are repetitive (thoughts you've had before) and over 80% are negative.[17] The heart of man is constantly feeding on spiritual Cheez-Its in today's culture. It tastes good on the tongue, but it's dietary asphalt for our heart. What you're feeding the mind through your eyes and ears every day affects you profoundly.

The New Testament warns us to *"Be sober-minded; be watchful. Your adversary the devil prowls around like a roaring lion, seeking someone to devour"* (1 Peter 5:8). A sober-minded man is clear-headed, rational, self-controlled. He's acutely aware of outside influences. He has sound judgment. He focuses on godly things. Philippians 4:8 tells us where our heart should find nourishment: *"whatever is true, whatever is honorable, whatever is right, whatever is pure, whatever is lovely, whatever is of good repute, if there is any excellence and if anything worthy of praise, dwell on these things."*

I gave up sugared beverages after my heart attack. I had a habit of drinking an entire 12-pack of Mountain Dew every few days. That's 46 grams of sugar per case, about 90% of the total weekly recommended amount of sugar. No wonder I was diabetic. I was flooding my body with garbage. But my spiritual heart was equally unhealthy. The TV shows and movies I watch, the online content I scrolled through, the music I listened to. Very little of it could survive if put through the filter of Philippians 4:8.

Every doctor will tell you breakfast is the most important meal of the day. And every pastor will tell you to start the day in God's Word and prayer. That's a spiritual breakfast. I used to do my Bible study time in the evening, but I switched it to the morning. I realized I wasn't beginning my day by feeding my spiritual heart. As a result, I consumed spiritual junk food the remainder of the day. I had not set my mind to *"whatever is true, honorable, right, pure"*. Men must guard their hearts by starting with a daily, good, hearty, spiritual breakfast.

Keep your shield up

The Sentinels at the Tomb of the Unknown Soldier don't carry shields, but warriors of old used to. Before guns, fighters carried a sword in one hand and a shield in the other. A shield is a great tool for protection. It blocks close-in attacks in hand-to-hand combat. It protects against longer-range weapons like spears and arrows. Today we wear helmets and bullet-proof vests, but the concept of a shield is the same. The Apostle Paul writes, *"In all circumstances take up the shield of faith, with which you can extinguish all the flaming darts of the evil one"* (Ephesians 6:16). The people who Paul wrote this to knew how to use a shield.

A MAN CANNOT SURROUND HIMSELF WITH PEOPLE OF ILL REPUTE AND EXPECT HIS HEART TO REMAIN PURE.

The Roman soldier's shield was called a *scutum*. It was made of wood and covered by an animal hide. It had metal trim on the edges. It was large, ranging about two to three feet wide and four to five feet long, about the size of a door. A man carried his shield because he always wanted to be ready to repel an attack. The Bible describes a shield as a spiritual tool related to faith. Faith is the understanding that God is Who He says He is and will keep His Word. Because we believe God, then we do the things God says to do, and not do, knowing God will keep His Word. A shield is a defensive weapon, so faith for the man is a defensive tool.

Our belief in God helps us to guard our heart. John 14:1 links these two ideas precisely. Jesus said, *"Let not your hearts be troubled. Believe in God; believe also in me."* Our trust and belief in God keeps our hearts from being anxious, worried, misdirected, apprehensive, uneasy. My thoughts go to action movies, right before the hero opens the door to jump in and save the day. He'll turn and say to the camera, "I have a bad feeling about this!" A man's heart, guarded by the shield of faith, can keep him from bad situations. We can ask ourselves, "Do I trust that God is in this? Do I trust He will keep His Word in this situation?" A man can look to God in uneasy situations, then turn to His Word and His promises. A man's heart may tell him, "I have a bad feeling about this!"

Keep your friends around
You can guard your heart not only by controlling what goes in it, and how you shield it, but also what you allow to surround it. The Bible is replete with teaching about the kind

of company we keep, and how it affects our own conviction and character. A man cannot surround himself with people of ill repute and expect his heart to remain pure. Psalm 1:1-3 teaches, *"Blessed is the man who walks not in the counsel of the wicked, nor stands in the way of sinners, nor sits in the seat of scoffers; but his delight is in the law of the Lord, and on his law he meditates day and night. He is like a tree planted by streams of water that yields its fruit in its season, and its leaf does not wither. In all that he does, he prospers."*

We are warned against three kinds of people—the wicked, the sinners and the scoffers. Notice the blessed man doesn't hang out with these people. He doesn't seek their counsel. He doesn't stand among them. He doesn't sit down with them. A straightforward way for a man to guard his heart against these companions is to surround himself with fellow Christ-followers. This is the benefit of a church family. The ministry in which I serve is a fellowship of Christian men. These small groups meet weekly at tables. They join together to *"delight in in the law of the Lord, and meditate on it day and night".*

When it comes to men, we are in a friendship recession. In a recent survey from the Center on American Life, only one in five men said they received emotional support from a friend in the last week.[18] The article explains, "'The falling off of friendships between men begins around middle and late adolescence and grows starker in adulthood,' said Judy Yi-Chung Chu, who teaches a class on boys' psychological development at Stanford University. 'Boys don't start emotionally disconnected; they become emotionally disconnected.'" True, meaningful friendships will not just occur for adult men. They must be sought and cultivated. A man who wants to guard his heart seeks out friendships that will be Sentinels in his life, keeping watch day and night for his spiritual wellbeing.

Keep your shoes on
I love the classic Kenny Rogers song, "The Gambler". He sings, "You gotta know when to walk away, and know when to run." Sometimes the way to preserve the heart is to just get up and run. You might believe that a real man should always stand and fight, but that's not what the Bible says, especially when it comes to sin.

The Bible tells us to flee from all kinds of things. We should run from youthful passions (2 Timothy 2:22). We should run from sexual immorality (1 Corinthians 6:18). We should run from the love of money and the desire to be rich (1 Timothy 6:11). We should flee idolatry (1 Corinthians 10:14). There are paths in life where you shouldn't stop to ask questions, or pick up a shield and stand guard. Instead, you should turn away and run for your life, as fast as you can. To guard your heart is to put distance between it and those acts and attitudes that can cause it damage.

In the Old Testament, Joseph had found favor with God. After his brothers sold him into slavery, he worked hard and became the chief attendant in the household of Potiphar, an Egyptian nobleman. Soon Potiphar's wife started noticing Joseph and said, *"Come to bed with me!" (Genesis 39:7)*. Joseph declined. She kept coming on to Joseph, day after day. But he refused to go to bed with her and eventually even refused to be in the same room with her.

One day Joseph found himself alone in the house attending to his duties when Potiphar's wife came into the room. She grabbed him by his coat and again demanded, *"Come to bed with me!"* Genesis records that Joseph *"left his cloak in her hand and ran out of the house" (Genesis 39:12).* Joseph had a simple answer to the temptation to sin that Potiphar's wife brought to him. He didn't fight, or stop to reason with her, or summon others to his aid. He just ran from it. Often the best choice for something that threatens our heart is not to think about it, but to run from it. The timeless wisdom of Kenny Rogers—"Know when to walk away, and know when to run!"

Growing in value

What happens to the heart when a man guards it well? The same thing that happens to anything of worth that we guard. It increases in value. As a man guards his heart, he grows closer to God and more in tune with His ways. His outward actions match up with his innermost thoughts, because as Proverbs 4:23 teaches, *"everything he does flows from it."* A well-guarded heart of great value results in a man of great value. Proverbs 27:19 reminds us, *"As in water face reflects face, so the heart of man reflects the man."*

If you want to know what kind of man you really are, look at your heart. What do you think about, put your time and talents to? What relationships to you value? What do your priorities and speech and conduct say about you? Have you fed your heart a healthy diet of thoughts and words, shielded it with unwavering faith, and surrounded it with people of great character? When your heart is under attack, do you have the good sense to pick up and run from immorality, idolatry and other sins?

Sometimes when a man fails through lack of effort or energy, we'll say, "His heart just wasn't in it." It's a shortcut to communicate that a man lacks passion, commitment. That he did not give his full and complete attention to it. When it comes to acting like a man, growing in manhood and leadership in all aspects of life and work, I have to sometimes ask myself, "Is my heart in it?" Am I putting my full energy to being the man God desires me to be? The heart of a man is a good bellwether as to his overall spiritual condition.

After my heart surgery I had a week or so in the cardiac unit at the hospital. As I laid in recovery, I had time to Google around on my phone. I learned that a person can survive for hours, even days, when their brain is inactive. If you are knocked unconscious, doctors can revive you some time later, and your brain can resume normal activity. The brain has a dormant state. I had a relative who was put into a medically-induced coma for 45 days, and came back with her full faculties.

The heart, on the other hand—you can go about two minutes after your heart stops beating before you die. It feeds blood to the body, and without it, you simply shut down. Lights out. Paramedics learn CPR not to keep the brain going, but to keep the blood moving through the body should the heart stop. The heart of man, your innermost being, is like your physical heart. Fail to guard it, and the man dies. With the heart of man, we must perceive it to be of infinite value. Like the Sentinels, we must keep watch over it day and night.

The walk of the guard:

- What are you feeding your heart today? From TV to websites to music, conversations, books, hobbies and habits, are they healthy for your heart or toxic?

- What is most valuable in your life and work? How are you guarding it to ensure it is protected and gives positive influence?

- What are some circumstances where you might need to flee if you encounter an attack on your heart?

- Which friends would you call on right now if you had an emotional or spiritual crisis? Consider investing in relationships in order to surround your heart with true friends.

A MAN FEARS

"Never fear to deliberately walk through dark places, for that is how you reach the light on the other side."
—Vernon Howard

The Grand Canyon Skywalk is a horseshoe shaped bridge that extends out over the edge of the Canyon. Walk out onto the Skywalk and you can experience an incredible vista, looking off a cliff more than 4,000 feet high to the riverbed below. Despite it's beautiful view, many people won't go near this modern engineering marvel. They're fearful because the floor of the Grand Canyon Skywalk is made of glass. There you stand, 70-feet out from the canyon wall, looking down through a thin sheet of glass from a height of 369 stories. It's like looking through the floor of an airplane without the plane. It gives even rock-steady men a sense of vertigo.

The Skywalk is entirely safe. Each pane of the glass floor is three inches thick, made of layers of incredibly strong glass that can individually support 800 people. The bridge itself can support the weight of more than seventy fully-loaded 747 aircraft. The $30 million structure took three years to build and contains more than 1.2 million pounds of steel and glass. It can withstand a magnitude 8.0 earthquake and winds of more than 100 miles per hour.[19] Despite all of that, many people approach the Grand Canyon Skywalk in abject terror, and simply aren't able to walk the transparent attraction for fear of falling.

Acrophobia is an irrational and persistent fear of heights. Less than 1% of men have acrophobia, though The Grand Canyon Skywalk is evidence of that statistic being off by a significant margin. About 10% of people suffer from a serious phobia.[20] Another 20% suffer from an anxiety disorder.[21] Lest you think fear is limited to a few people, you only have to consider glossophobia, which is fear of public speaking. That affects roughly 75% of all adults. Fear is something that's built into our psyche. All men experience it in one way or another. There are books and courses on overcoming fear. But the Bible gives us an interesting perspective on fear and its importance for a men.

Born with it
Some fears men are born with and some are learned. Research shows that innate fears include predators, pain, heights, rapidly approaching objects and ancestral threats like snakes and spiders.[22] Our body is constructed by God with a built-in mechanism to protect us. This automatic physiological reaction is called "fight or flight" response, and

THE BIBLE SAYS
FEAR IS THE
RESULT OF SIN.
WHEN ADAM DISOBEYED
GOD IN THE GARDEN,
HE HID IN FEAR.

it is a combination of the body identifying an innate fear, and then reacting through either fighting it or fleeing.

In his 1915 book *Bodily Changes in Pain, Hunger, Fear and Rage,* physiologist Walter Bradford Cannon noted that when we are threatened, our bodies all have similar responses, including releasing of adrenaline, cortisol and epinephrine, increased heart rate and respiration, increased blood flow to muscles, eye dilation, and the liver delivering more glucose to the muscles and brain.[23] The body prepares automatically and without our input to quickly react and protect itself from danger. Put your hand on a hot stove or in an electrical socket, and your arm instantly pulls away. Or hear a noise in the house late at night, and you immediately reach for a heavy object and your eyes adjust to see more clearly in the dark.

As men, we manifest common fears that come with age and experience. Some of the fears we might gain include:
- Being unable to afford living expenses or medical treatments
- Being dependent on others
- Being the victim of abuse or a crime or feeling defenseless or unsafe in a situation
- A loved one becoming seriously ill or dying
- Being left alone, or isolated from family
- Loss of dignity or self-esteem because of issues that naturally occur as you mature.[24]

Where does fear come from? The Bible says that our fear is the result of sin. When Adam disobeyed God in the Garden of Eden, he hid in fear—this is the first time fear is ever mentioned. Genesis 3:8-10 recounts, *"Then the man and his wife heard the sound of the Lord God as he was walking in the garden in the cool of the day, and they hid from the Lord God among the trees of the garden. But the Lord God called to the man, 'Where are you?' He answered, 'I heard you in the garden, and I was afraid because I was naked; so I hid.'"*

Throughout the Bible we see examples of fear. Moses was afraid when God told him to confront Pharaoh. The Israelites were afraid of giants that were living in the Promised Land. Jonah was afraid when God told him to go to Nineveh. Elijah feared Queen Jezebel. Fear of men and earthly troubles that we face was common in Bible times all the way through our time. Men's greatest fears now tend to focus on what others might do to them—pain or loss we may suffer as a result of our actions or inactions.

Men have nothing to fear

Though fear was not present in God's perfect creation, once it came about, God uses this strong emotional and physical reaction for our benefit. First, God tells us not to fear. Isaiah 41:10 tells us, *"Fear not, for I am with you; be not dismayed, for I am your God; I will strengthen you, I will help you, I will uphold you with my righteous right hand."* The phrase "fear not" appears 302 times in Scripture; "Do not be afraid" appears 33 times, "Do not fear" appears 66 times; "Do not be dismayed" is written 99 times. It is the most repeated command in the Bible. Not a request or suggestion, but a command by God. When it comes to obeying God and contemplating the negative consequences possible by the hands of men, we are instructed over and over, do not fear. Why should men "fear not" when it comes to God?

God's presence goes with us. We might fear that we are isolated by a situation or circumstance—that we face a difficulty alone. But God is always with us. Joshua 1:9 says, *"Have I not commanded you? Be strong and courageous. Do not be afraid; do not be discouraged, for the Lord your God will be with you wherever you go."* In Deuteronomy 31:6, God says, *"Do not be afraid or terrified because of them, for the Lord your God goes with you; he will never leave you nor forsake you."* The presence of God gives us confidence to face our fears.

God's promises are for us. Scripture promises that when we trust God, He keeps us safe. Proverbs 29:25 says, *"The fear of man lays a snare, but whoever trusts in the Lord is safe."* Jesus Himself promised with regard to His disciples fearing persecution, *"But don't be afraid of those who threaten you. For the time is coming when everything that is covered will be revealed, and all that is secret will be made known to all"* (Matthew 10:26). Jesus promises that as we endure difficulty, in the end we will be proven right and the motives of those against Christ will be exposed.

God's peace is upon us. In our challenges and troubles, God provides His peace. This is an innate sense that God is working for our good and His glory, so we can be calm and collected in fearful circumstances. John 16:33 says, *"I have told you these things, so that in me you may have peace. In this* *world you will have trouble. But take heart! I have overcome the world."* What things has God told us? We know about Jesus, and we know the "end of the story", what happens to the earth and all that we fear. Because we know these things we can have peace that God is in control and nothing that happens is unexpected to Him.

God's protection is around us. Just as we have an autonomic nervous system that protects our bodies automatically when threatened, we have a spiritual mechanism given to us by God to allay our fears. 2 Timothy 1:7 confirms, *"God gave us a spirit not of fear but of power and love and self-control."* We are not left to face our challenges with fear and timidity. Paul is writing to his protégé Timothy as one who has been abandoned by his friends, attacked by his foes and left alone in a Roman prison. Yet Paul writes that he is not fearful in his suffering. This is not a pep-talk or Paul saying that Timothy needs to have a certain mindset. Instead, we are equipped with God's Holy Spirit, the power of God Himself to guide our thoughts, actions and relationships. Spirit-produced power enables us to endure suffering and to abound in hope in whatever circumstances we face (2 Timothy 1:8, Romans 15:13).[25]

God's provision is given to us. Psalm 23 is a great song about God's provision through fear and difficulties. Psalm 23:4 says, *"Even though I walk through the valley of the shadow of death, I will fear no evil, for you are with me; your rod and your staff, they comfort me."* The rod and staff are instruments that a shepherd uses to guide his sheep. Psalm

WE MIGHT FEAR THAT WE ARE ISOLATED BY A SITUATION OR CIRCUMSTANCE—THAT WE FACE A DIFFICULTY ALONE. BUT GOD IS ALWAYS WITH US.

23 begins, *"The Lord is my shepherd, I lack nothing..."* (Psalm 23:1). The picture given is of someone walking through a fearful situation, and God as shepherd providing for their needs, pulling them back with the staff when they wander off the right path, pushing them forward with the rod when they aren't moving.

Psalm 23:8 says, *"You prepare a table before me in the presence of my enemies."* This is an interesting illustration, but not of God preparing a banquet party before an enemy army. Here the table is that of a negotiation, the idea of diplomats meeting. The Psalmist is saying that even as we have fear of those who are aligned against us, God is preparing to negotiate peace on our behalf, to restore the relationship and bring friendship from fear.

Men have everything to fear
Which is it? Should men live fearlessly, or should men instead be afraid? And afraid of what, if so? In Genesis 3 we read that God walked in the Garden of Eden before man sinned. There was friendship between God and man. Yet after sin, the relationship markedly changed. As soon as man sinned and encountered God, Adam says in Genesis 3:10, *"I heard you in the garden, and I was afraid..."* Though later in the Bible God tells man not to fear, on this first encounter, that's not how God responds.

Adam had reason to fear. God had said to him, *"You must not eat fruit from the tree that is in the middle of the garden, and you must not touch it, or you will die"* (Genesis 3:3). Did Adam fear death? Did he even know what death was? And why, if fear enters the world because of Adam's sin, does God then begin using fear through history? Do we to fear God because of sin, or fear God as a part of our relationship with Him and to know Him more fully?

To better understand the fear of the Lord, we should get a handle on what the word fear means. In the Old Testament when reading of the fear God, the word used is *yirah*, Hebrew most often translated as "awe, respect and reverence". However, *yirah* also denotes "trembling and terror". In Exodus 20, God gave Moses the Ten Commandments on Mount Sinai while the people of Israel watched from below. When Moses came down from the mountain, Exodus 20:18-19 says, *"When the people saw the thunder and lightning and heard the trumpet and saw the mountain in smoke, they trembled with fear. They stayed at a distance and said to Moses, 'Speak to us yourself and we will listen. But do not have God speak to us or we will die.'"* The people had seen God's presence on the mountain and there is no doubt this was not a reaction of just respect or awe, they were truly terrified. The word used is *yirah*.

Don't be afraid—but be very afraid. Moses responds, *"Do not be afraid. God has come to test you, so that the fear of God will be with you to keep you from sinning"* (Exodus 20:20). Here we see the same base word used twice. Don't be afraid (*yare:* to fear)... the fear (*yirah:* a fear) of God will be with you...[26] Is this teaching contradictory? Don't fear God, but at the same time, fear God? In a sense, yes, both are true.

The Bible is teaching us what a healthy fear of God is. When the people were terrified in God's presence, Moses is saying that we do not need to be afraid of the very presence of God, but we do need to have a healthy fear of disobeying or disrespecting God.

There is a difference between *being afraid* and *having fear.* Imagine you are standing near a jet engine that is running. You would be in awe of the raw power it produces. It would be incredibly loud. The thrust would be impressive, the high-speed compressor spinning at 9,000 rpm, able to propel a plane weighing more than 100 tons through the air at 500 miles per hour. At the same time, you would be wise to fear standing too close, lest you get sucked in and killed by its lethal force. Jet engines can consume nearly 2,900 pounds of air per second. The engine, if not respected, could kill you instantly. When you board an airplane, sit by a window and look out to see the engine, you don't fear it, and run in terror for the terminal. You realize its purpose, its potential, its function, and have a healthy respect for it. But you would not dare stand in front of it. This balanced combination of awe and terror is the word *fear* applied to God.

According to Scripture, the healthy and holy fear of God is more clearly realized for us in the New Testament. As Christians, we live with Christ in us, and He has forgiven our sins against God. So, we need no longer fear the penalty for our sin, which is both physical and eternal death. At the same time, we have an awe, reverence and respect for Almighty God and a desire to please Him. We have an awareness of His power and might. Jesus makes this distinction when talking about fear with His disciples. In Luke 12:4-5 Jesus says, *"I tell you, my friends, do not be afraid of those who kill the body and after that can do no more. But I will show you whom you should fear: Fear him who, after your body has been killed, has authority to throw you into hell. Yes, I tell you, fear him."* The New Testament word for fear being used here, in the original Greek, is *phobethete*. It means to be terrified, frightened and to be in reverence of.

In Christ, men have everything to fear. As we develop a healthy fear of God, that sense of reverence, awe and respect guides our thoughts and actions. Scripture consistently connects our fear of God to living smart. Proverbs 9:10 says, *"The fear of the Lord is the beginning of wisdom, and knowledge of the Holy One is understanding."*

Fear of God sustains us. When we have a relationship with God through Jesus Christ, our fear of God is not for His judgment. Rather, our fear is of being distant or separated from Him. A healthy fear of God draws us closer to Him and moves us to take refuge in Him. Psalm 31:19 teaches, *"Oh, how abundant is your goodness, which you have stored up for those who fear you and worked for those who take refuge in you, in the sight of the children of mankind!"* The writer is saying that, when it comes to God, our greatest fear should be living outside of His guidance, greatness and protection.[27] As a man, do you fear living apart from the guidance and protection of God? Scripture warns the walk of manhood is a lonely and dangerous one without Christ by our side.

Does it seem a little self-centered of God to desire our singular devotion to Him? God commands us, *"You shall not make for yourself an idol in the form of anything in heaven above or on the earth beneath or in the waters below. You shall not bow down to them or worship them; for I, the Lord your God, am a jealous God..." (Exodus 20:4-5).* This is not jealousy in the human sense—desiring something that does not belong to us. No, God is saying that He does not want us giving anything else the devotion and respect that rightfully belongs to Him.[28] This reverence, the fear of the Lord, is shown in how a man conducts his life and work.

A profound relationship. Reverence for God is an intense and earnest respect and love for Him. More than an internal feeling, reverence is something that is outwardly demonstrated through actions. We honor God, we express gratitude to Him. We obey His commands and teachings. We pray to Him, and we learn about Him through His Word. We approach God with humility and in the manner God prescribes. If we truly fear God, people around us will see this in how we live our lives. 1 Peter 1:17 reminds us, *"And if you call on him as Father who judges impartially according to each one's deeds, conduct yourselves with fear..."*

The promise of fear
Scripture does tell us to fear God, but there are promises we can claim as we develop and live by this healthy fear:

Fear of God makes life go well: *"Oh that they had such a heart as this always, to fear me and to keep all my* commandments, that it might go well with them and with their descendants forever" (Deuteronomy 5:29)!

Fear of God results in His compassion: *"As a father shows compassion to his children, so the Lord shows compassion to those who fear him" (Psalm 103:13).*

Fear of God gives us confidence: *"In the fear of the Lord one has strong confidence, and his children will have a refuge" (Proverbs 14:26).*

Fear of God results in blessing: *"Blessed is the man who fears the Lord, who greatly delights in his commandments!" (Psalm 112:1).*

Fear of God keeps us from sin: *"Moses said to the people, 'Do not fear, for God has come to test you, that the fear of him may be before you, that you may not sin'" (Exodus 20:20).*

Fear of God makes us holy: *"Since we have these promises, beloved, let us cleanse ourselves from every defilement of body and spirit, bringing holiness to completion in the fear of God" (2 Corinthians 7:1).*

Fear of God is evidence of our salvation: *"Therefore, my beloved, as you have always obeyed, so now, not only as in my presence but much more in my absence, work out your own salvation with fear and trembling, for it is God who works in you, both to will and to work for his good pleasure" (Philippians 2:12-13).*

Fear of God results in our needs being fulfilled: *"Oh, fear the Lord, you his saints, for those who fear him have no lack!"* (Psalm 34:9).

Fear of God makes Him our friend: *"The friendship of the Lord is for those who fear him, and he makes known to them his covenant"* (Psalm 25:14).

Fear of God leads to life: *"The fear of the Lord leads to life. Whoever has it rests satisfied; he will not be visited by harm"* (Proverbs 19:23).

Fear of God fulfills His requirement for us: *"And now, Israel, what does the Lord your God require of you, but to fear the Lord your God, to walk in all his ways, to love him, to serve the Lord your God with all your heart and with all your soul..."* (Deuteronomy 10:12).

Fear of God grants us His mercy: *"And his mercy is for those who fear him from generation to generation"* (Luke 1:50).

Fear and trust are related

I would never walk the Grand Canyon Skywalk. Despite no issue at all flying on an airplane, I have a fear of heights. I don't like roller coasters. Or ladders. I'm particularly afraid of glass elevators. Flying along at 30,000 feet doesn't frighten me, but between 10 feet and 30,000 feet makes me queasy.

When I was around 10 years old, my dad bought a condominium in Panama City Beach, Florida, to rent out

AS WE DEVELOP A HEALTHY FEAR OF GOD, THAT SENSE OF REVERENCE, AWE AND RESPECT GUIDES OUR THOUGHTS AND ACTIONS.

to vacationers. The side benefit was that the family would occasionally go down to spend a week or a weekend at the beach. The condo was on the fourteenth floor, and when you exited the elevator, there was a long walkway to the door of our unit. The aluminum railing of the walk looked flimsy, and you could see through the rungs all the day down those fourteen floors to the parking lot below. I was so scared. I felt like I was walking on a tightrope from the elevator to the condo. I would press myself against the wall of the building opposite the railing, and not look down. I would keep my eyes straight ahead and gently scoot along to the door. If it was windy or rainy, that was an extra measure of terror. Whenever we were in the car on the way to the condo, I would start thinking about that high-wire walk to the door from the elevator, hours in advance.

Once at the condo, dad asked me to take the trash to the trash chute. I couldn't do it. Walking *with a bag in my hand* all the way down to the chute, which was basically a hole in the wall dropping to the ground floor? Are you kidding me!?

One summer we went to the condo and stayed for a week. I remember something happening during that trip. The first three days, I was doing my fear-walk to the condo each day. Then around day four, I began to get used to the walk. I had made it a dozen or more times, and to my amazement, the concrete walkway held, the railing didn't fall off, and I didn't fall to my death from a great height. I was still fearful of the high walkway, but I had started to trust it. The more I walked, the less I feared. By the end of the week I was even going over to the railing and looking down, admiring the view. I wasn't going to fall to my death from the fourteenth floor.

Fear and trust have an interesting relationship. When you fear something, but you continue to interact with it, over time you can grow to trust it. If I never took that walkway, or the condo was on the first floor, then I would have never grown to trust it and get comfortable walking on the fourteenth floor. I might apply this same thought to God. If I fear Him, but continue to interact with Him, over time my trust in Him will grow. Healthy respect, awe and reverence can result in greater trust, over time.

The Bible instructs man to develop a healthy fear (respect, reverence, awe, terror) of God. When we have this fear, then we tend not to have phobias and anxieties related to our fellow man. Fear of God helps us to build trust in God. Psalm 56:3-4 sings, *"When I am afraid, I put my trust in you. In God, whose word I praise—in God I trust and am not afraid. What can mere mortals do to me?"*

Fear of God also helps us to overcome fears related to our fellow man—to live courageously when it comes to life and work. Joshua 1:9 says, *"Have I not commanded you? Be strong and courageous. Do not be terrified; do not be discouraged, for the Lord your God will be with you wherever you go."* Do you lead courageously and with strength of character and purpose? If you are following God you can lead a life undaunted. Fear, so you don't fear—seemingly contradictory instructions, but helping us to trust and obey God.

FEAR AND TRUST HAVE AN INTERESTING RELATIONSHIP. WHEN YOU FEAR SOMETHING, BUT YOU CONTINUE TO INTERACT WITH IT, OVER TIME YOU CAN GROW TO TRUST IT.

When we fear God, we appreciate His character, we are moved to believing and trusting Him, and we develop concern for disobeying God, and so being subjected to God's justice. Proverbs 9:10 says, *"The fear of the Lord is the beginning of wisdom, and knowledge of the Holy One is understanding."* Awe and submission to God, then, is a fear that brings us wisdom, knowledge and understanding. When we understand the fear of God, then we can lead a fearless life.

The walk of fear:

- *What fears do you have that are of other men or circumstances in your life or work? Do you believe that God protects you from these?*

- *Do you have a healthy fear of God? Do you consider what happens when you displease or disobey Him? How do you show an awe and reverence for God through your life activities?*

- *How are you growing to trust God more over time?*

A MAN FATHERS

*"You cannot teach a
crab to walk straight."*
—Aristophanes

Don't skip this

Please, don't jump over this chapter if you are not a dad, thinking, "This doesn't apply to me." It does, in two important ways. First, all men have some aspect of fatherhood in their lives, whether it's supervising employees, or mentoring another man, or sharing wisdom, or serving others. All men are also created in God's image, and God is our Heavenly Father. There are lessons to be learned by every man when considering the "father" we are to those around us.

Second, even if you are not a dad, you *have* a dad or you *had* a dad. You wouldn't exist without him. He may be alive and you know him well, or he passed away a while ago, or he walked out when you were five. Who you are right now is heavily influenced by your father. Every son picks up aspects of his life, work and character from his father, whether you like it or not. You'll know more about yourself by learning about fatherhood and God's expectation of it. So read on.

A walk in Wuhan

My wife and I stepped off the bus along with three other couples. We stood in front of a nondescript office building. We could see the lobby before us through the glass entrance doors. It was a typically summer day in Wuhan, China. Yes, the same city where the coronavirus originated—but this happened years earlier. The sun baked the concrete parking lot. It felt like the soles of my shoes would melt on it. I held my video camera to capture the occasion. We started walking.

It had rained the night before, so the air was atypically clear. The humidity was so high I could have held up a sponge and wrung water out of the thick air. The walk was hot. I was ready to move inside, but that would give only shade. The Chinese rarely turned on the air conditioning, as power to cool the whole building was too expensive.

Our guide in the lead, we walked into the building, then up the curving lobby stairs covered in thick red carpet to the second floor. We walked single-file, a group of four families. The lights were off, again to conserve power, but there was plenty of illumination from the lobby windows. We shuffled our heels down the terrazzo-floored hallway through a nondescript wooden door and into a large room. Here the air conditioner unit in the corner had been turned on for our group. I felt a blast of comfort as I walked through the threshold.

On the other side of the room were several seated women, each holding a small child. And there she was, our soon-to-be daughter. I recognized her from the photos we can been provided ahead of our trip. She was just 18 months old. She had a round head and face and short black hair that hugged her head. Her almond-shaped eyes were a deep, dark brown. She was nervous, more so that a crowd of several American families—all strangers talking in gibberish—had just walked into the room. She gripped her caregiver and buried her head in her sleeve.

Adopting a child was really my wife's idea. Keri and I had only been married a year or so, but we married later than our parents, I was 35 and she was 31. So, we had already had a lot of adulthood behind us and were both ready to start a family. We were deeply involved in our church, which had a culture of foster care and adoption provided by a number of family ministries. I had just completed a local mission project, renovating the home of a foster mother with a bunch of kids she was caring for. Keri, my wife, had traveled to Ukraine and ministered to orphan children there. She came back with the adoption bug and so we met with a local agency and started walking that path.

It's different to foster or adopt than it is to have a biological child. When your wife finds out she's pregnant, the deal is sealed. The sex is decided by God, the timetable is determined. You buy and assemble the crib, have a baby shower, mark your calendar, get ready for the day. With adoption, though, you're in control of more. You choose the age of the child, the

ALL MEN HAVE SOME ASPECT OF FATHERHOOD IN THEIR LIVES, WHETHER IT'S SUPERVISING EMPLOYEES, OR MENTORING ANOTHER MAN, OR SHARING WISDOM, OR SERVING OTHERS.

sex. If you'd rather have a girl you can tell the agency "We want a girl." In our case with international adoption we chose the nationality, based on which nations the United States had a relationship with for the purpose of matching parents and children.

With adoption there's training involved. We got a ton of information on attachment and bonding, health and diet, and all the things I just assumed that someone told every parent. Surely, they pull pregnant moms aside at some point before you go into the delivery room and give you a full set of instructions, some kind of owner's manual? There were classes to attend and approvals to file. We took seminars and watched videos and read books. We had background checks, gave personal references, and prepared a portfolio of our marriage. A social worker came to inspect our home.

We chose to adopt from China. At the time there were thousands of children in China, Ukraine, Uganda, Honduras—lots of countries—who were orphaned and in need of parents. China had a straightforward system run by their government and so it was predictable for us in terms of time and cost. A stateside adoption agency organized the whole thing, which took a few years from kickoff to kid.

The point is that I had a lot of time to not only think about fatherhood, but to prepare ahead of time to become a dad, with tons of experts to call on for help. In our case the process of our first adoption took 22 months because of some procedural delays. Now here we were, walking into the civil affairs office in Wuhan, China, on an ordinary weekday. During the walk up the stairs is when it hit me that despite all the time and training for fatherhood, I was woefully unprepared.

Then, poof!
One by one, each couple went to the desk at the front of the room. They called us by last name. Our interpreter and guide helped us fill out the next round of paperwork. There was plenty of paperwork—some before we left for China, some once we arrived, some today, more to come. All in Chinese, with translations attached, sign here, initial here. A smile, a handshake.

And there she was. A caregiver came over and put little Eden into Keri's waiting arms. They both started crying. I tried to get a few pictures and some video to remember the moment. We invited Keri's mom along for the trip and she was there with her camera snapping away and smiling. We called her the Nana-razzi. Like the celebrity paparazzi, she was always camera-in-hand, ready to get a good picture.

I walked off the bus ten minutes ago married with a job and few commitments beyond my wife, a house, and some monthly payments. Then, poof! Instantly I was a father. Now I had real responsibility! We had skipped all the newborn sleeping and cooing and teething. This girl was already walking and talking and partially potty-trained. A little person was going to be depending on me. I kept thinking, "Surely someone is going to go over our paperwork and ask some questions." Like getting a driver license—wasn't there some kind of parenting test? An eye exam? The walk *to* fatherhood had been about 200 yards. The walk *of* fatherhood, though, would take many, many years.

Only a man can father
There are practical aspects to being a dad. Moms tend to handle much of the emotional support. Dads, though, are the risk takers and the rule makers. They tend to push kids to try new things. And they set the foundation for what's acceptable in the home. Fathers also parent children somewhat similarly to how they were raised. I can see that. Much of my personality and the way I interact with my kids comes from how I interacted with my own dad.

Fatherhood is something only a man can do. Single moms can raise children, and I don't take anything away from those who have that difficult task. But without the father, there's an element missing. A mom can't be a dad, and vice-versa. A father is uniquely equipped by God to be the spiritual leader of the home. When Joshua declares, *"But as for me and my house, we will serve the Lord" (Joshua 24:15),* he is setting the spiritual tone and priority for his family.

Fatherless men
As of 2023, about 20% of US children live without a father in the home—around 18.3 million kids.[29] A recent study found children in a fatherless home are more likely to suffer from mental health and behavioral problems, and are generally less successful at school. For girls, those that had no father

in the home are eight times more likely to get pregnant as a teenager. Children without fathers in the home are 279% more likely to carry a gun or deal drugs than those living with their fathers.[30]

This doesn't mean kids without fathers at home are doomed. But men should acknowledge if their father wasn't around growing up, it has affected them, mentally, personally and spiritually. How a man relates to other men, how he values and treats women, the work and life ethic he grows into, the way he leads—all of these facets of development are most heavily influenced by his father. If dad wasn't around, or was himself dysfunctional, then his sons and daughters may have a skewed understanding in one or more of these areas that is affecting them as adults.

Like it or not
A child is going to learn from his or her father whether dad likes it or not. Kids are built to observe, ask, experience and copy. We can't choose what a child learns from us anymore than we could teach a crab to walk straight. The way our kids see us and emulate what they see is baked-in. If we want godly children, we have to be godly fathers. Just as God said of Abraham, *"For I have chosen him, so that he will direct his children and his household after him to keep the way of the Lord by doing what is right and just, so that the Lord will bring about for Abraham what He has promised him"* (Genesis 18:19).

The picture Abraham paints is a man who directs his children toward God by example, and then God bringing about His

HOW A MAN RELATES TO OTHER MEN, HOW HE VALUES AND TREATS WOMEN, HIS WORK AND LIFE ETHIC, THE WAY HE LEADS—
ALL OF THESE ARE HEAVILY INFLUENCED BY HIS FATHER.

blessing to Abraham through them. As a father, realize that God may choose to bless your family not by your work or effort, but *through your children*. Often men try to make a name for themselves through their career, not realizing their greatest legacy will be their children, not their 401K. We can view fatherhood as one of many aspects of our lives, versus a primary and high-order priority—just as God chose Abraham to *"direct his children and his household after him."* How then, might a man approach the walk of godly fatherhood?

A man of Scripture
Abraham's example to *"command his children and his household after him to keep the way of the Lord"* is accomplished primarily through the Scriptures. Men should obey Ephesians 6:4 and *"...bring them up in the discipline and instruction of the Lord."* These two facets—discipline and instruction—are communicated to us in the Bible. Children that hear, read, discuss and pray the Scriptures in the home will be shepherded toward a God-directed life. The goal of a father isn't for his children to believe what dad says about God, but to learn to believe God for themselves.

Scripture helps a father to produce a child who trusts in God. 2 Timothy 3:16-17 teaches that *"All Scripture is breathed out by God and profitable for teaching, for reproof, for correction, and for training in righteousness, that the man of God may be complete, equipped for every good work."* The Scriptures prepare our children to do good works with their lives. God speaks through His Word and helps the parent discipline, correct and train their kids. When children hear the

Scriptures from their dad, they begin to develop their own love and trust in God's Word.

My dad was a Christian. He was involved in the church when I was growing up. He served as an usher, then as a deacon. Our family attended worship together every Sunday. We sat on the fourth row in the center section on the right-hand aisle, regular as clockwork. But dad didn't read the Scriptures to us. He led a Sunday School class, but never shared what he was teaching or learning with my brother or me. He would rather talk about politics or football instead of something he read in Romans or a story from the Old Testament. He engaged in the Scriptures for himself, and not for his family. He missed this opportunity of fatherhood.

I didn't develop a love for God's Word until I was in my 30s. I don't blame my dad for my lack of spiritual development. But I wonder how I may have grown and developed differently if our household were saturated in the Word of God. One thing I did learn from my dad is that just taking the family to church isn't a father's full responsibility for spiritual development. God must be talked about, prayed with, and acted upon, as a family, led by the father in the home. This is what the Bible means when Abraham *"command his children and his household after him to keep the way of the Lord".*

A man who models
The reality of fatherhood is that I can give my kids all of the instruction and precepts and virtuous truths I want to, but ultimately they're going to follow one thing when it comes

CONSIDER HOW WE TELL OUR KIDS THAT GOD IS OUR "HEAVENLY FATHER". WHAT IF THEY THINK, "IF GOD THE FATHER IS ANYTHING LIKE MY DAD, I DON'T WANT ANYTHING TO DO WITH HIM!?"

to me, and that is the example that I set for them. They're honestly not listening to most of what I say. They're looking at the way I act, because my actions are telling them what is important to me. A Christian psychologist once told me to make a list of "house rules" for my children. I thought about it, and realized it would be far more effective to make a list of house rules for myself, and live those out before my children. They will more readily pick up what I do, versus what I say.

Every father has the experience where they say something in front of their child that they regret. It might have been a moment of anger, or frustration, or a comment about someone else that you didn't think they'd catch or understand. Then, a few days later, that word or comment comes out of your child's mouth—and at the worst possible time.

Early on, when my son Levi was maybe 3 or 4, I got upset trying to assemble a toy that he was excited about. He sat next to me in rapt attention waiting for me to put all the segments together. It was one of those toys where the box looks big enough that I assumed it was in one piece, but down in the fine print at the bottom it said, "Some assembly required". I think the marketing people purposefully place these notes so they are only read after purchase. The toy came with that tiny Allen wrench that is not adequate for the job. That tool was only going to be used for 30 minutes in it's entire life, but it was determined by the manufacturer to make that time as frustrating as possible. It kept slipping out of the bolt I was trying to screw in. As I fumbled with the wrench, the bolt dropped to the floor and rolled under the table. I'd had it and hissed, "Shit!"

Levi laughed as I bent down to look for the bolt and said it back instantly: "Shit!" in his little toddler Levi voice. "Oh crap!" I thought, followed instantly by *don't say oh crap too! He'll pick that up as well.* Levi picked up a host of other words he's said from time to time. I'm not the only source with respect to language. Every time I hear something inappropriate come out of his mouth, I'll think that I very well may have taught him that in a moment of poor judgment.

More recently my children have begun to comment on my driving. My wife drove a school bus for a few years, so she became very conscientious about driving, always using her mirrors, constantly aware of her surroundings. These days from the back seat I'll hear, "Too fast, dad!", or "Use your turn signal!" The other day someone in front of me at the red light didn't move, so I honked my horn. My daughter said over my shoulder, "Set a good example dad!"

In Deuteronomy 11:18-20, Moses instructs the Israelites about the commandments of God: *"Fix these words of Mine in your hearts and minds; tie them as symbols on your hands and bind them on your foreheads. Teach them to your children, talking about them when you sit at home and when you walk along the road, when you lie down, and when you get up. Write them on the doorframes of your houses and on your gates."* Notice "teach God's Word to your children" is immediately followed by, *"when you sit at home, when you walk along the road, when you lie down, and when you get up."* The clear intent here is that a man should model God's Word, not just say it. A man must ask himself not only "Am I reading God's Word daily?" but also, "Am I modeling what God is teaching me?" If you want your kids to live as Christ-followers, then you'll need to do far more than know how to share the Gospel with them. You will need to be a *picture of the Gospel* they can see each day. This is the walk of fatherhood.

Here's a scary thought: The most important reason a man must serve as a model in fatherhood is the spiritual connection of their children to their *Father* God in heaven. Consider how we tell our kids that God is our "Heavenly Father", and throughout Scripture we read about God as Supreme and Creator—who is also a Father with a Son. If my relationship with my child is tattered, torn, distant, unremarkable, what thoughts will he or she apply to their Heavenly Father based on their relationship with their earthly father? May it not be so that my son or daughter would think, "If God the Father is anything like my dad, then I don't want anything to do with Him!"

A man who prays
How often do you pray about and for your children? In my experience, most men, if they pray, spend time praying about themselves, even if they are married. They pray about work, direction, goals, finances, relationships and health and other needs. But once they become fathers, their prayer shifts to their children. I pray for and about my children constantly. I didn't use to be a person of constant prayer. When my

thoughts go to one of them during the day, I'll pray a one or two sentence prayer to God about them.

I couldn't tell you where all of my kids are at any given time. I put Apple Airtags in their backpacks so I could track them. My oldest daughter got upset when I put an Airtag in the glove compartment of her car. "Don't you trust me?" she asked. Of course I trust her—or I wouldn't have let her have a car. But I'm concerned for her. I pray about my daughter's life-direction and relationships. For my middle child, I pray about her growing into maturity and making wise choices. For my youngest, I pray about him governing his emotions and receiving good input from all of the influences around him. I'm concerned for my kids because I realize I am but one of many influences on them.

Remember Philippians 4:6-7: *"Do not be anxious about anything, but in everything by prayer and supplication with thanksgiving let your requests be made known to God. And the peace of God, which surpasses all understanding, will guard your hearts and your minds in Christ Jesus."* Some of the ways I pray for my children, along with Scriptures that God provides to go with my thoughts, are:

God, may my children do good things in your eyes. *"Trust in the Lord; do good; dwell in the land and befriend faithfulness"* (Psalm 37:3).

God, I pray my children will have love and compassion for others. *"Love one another with brotherly affection. Outdo one another in showing honor"* (Romans 12:10).

God, please reveal my children's sins to them so they will know when they are doing wrong. *"For the Lord disciplines the one he loves, and chastises every son whom he receives"* (Hebrews 12:6).

God, may my children trust in You. *"I will extol You, my God, O King, And I will bless Your name forever and ever"* (Psalm 145:1).

God, may my children find their identity for life in Jesus. *"For we are his workmanship, created in Christ Jesus for good works, which God prepared beforehand, that we should walk in them"* (Ephesians 2:10).

God, I pray my children will listen to Your voice. *"My sheep hear my voice, and I know them, and they follow me. I give them eternal life, and they will never perish, and no one will snatch them out of my hand"* (John 10:27-28).

God, may my children make wise choices. *"So, whether you eat or drink, or whatever you do, do all to the glory of God"* (1 Corinthians 10:31).

A prayer chain

My son Levi was drug-exposed in the womb. He came to our family as a foster child, straight out of the NICU, where he had been weened off of drugs after his premature birth. He's grown into a smart, energetic, funny and fun-filled boy. I can hardly keep up. But his prenatal drug exposure affects his brain development. This most often impacts his decision-

THIS IS THE GREAT DEMAND OF FATHERHOOD—PUTTING ASIDE YOUR LIFE AND PRIORITIES FOR TIME WITH YOUR CHILDREN. DO IT EARLY AND OFTEN. THERE IS NO SUCH THING AS "MAKE UP TIME".

making. He gets anxious, and impatient. Sometimes he gets angry. Little disappointments and disagreements can blow up quickly. A few times he's thrown glass objects at me or my wife, and even punched a few holes in the walls.

During one particularly bad episode, when he was up in his room destroying toys, I texted a few men I knew and asked them to pray for him. After a while, Levi settled down. I realized that although I was praying for my son, I had all of these other people in my circle who would be happy to pray for him if I just asked. Why hadn't I done this before? After all, prayer works! Don't just pray for your children and family, involve others and ask them to pray as well. A father who prays gives his family over to a God Who cares and is working for our good.

I kept that prayer text thread. Every so often I send out a prayer request for Levi. I always get a response from these men who stop to pray for him. It's like having a spiritual militia at the ready. Right how I'm especially praying for Levi's salvation. He doesn't know the Lord, and coming to Christ is all about giving up control, turning it over to Him. That's going to be especially hard for Levi. He's all about being in control. But if he is going to begin a relationship with Christ, it will be, in part, because of all of the men around him who are praying for him.

Every man a mentor
There is a mentoring aspect to fatherhood. As my kids started to go from toddlers to elementary age, I realized there

were things I wanted them to know about life. Importantly I wanted them to know how to solve disagreements, how to treat others with respect, and how to love one another. Now that my two older children are beginning to make more of their own decisions, I want them to make wise choices, especially in their friend circle, and how they choose to invest their time.

I failed as many dads have before me. I did not intentionally set aside time when my kids were young to talk to them about important matters in life. I was at all of their sports events cheering them on. I was Mr. Carpool getting them from here to there. I was great at the provider role, making sure everyone had food and clothes and wifi, and the electric bill got paid. But I missed some excellent mentoring opportunities along the way—times when I should have taken one of them aside, sat down, and talked about choices I made, things I could have done better, and the opportunities they now had in front of them. They could have learned from me and done better.

Fatherhood is designed to allow a man to pass down his knowledge and experience from one generation to the next. This role is built-in—but a dad must take advantage of it! Remember Psalm 78:4, *"We will not hide them [God's words] from their children; we will tell the next generation the praiseworthy deeds of the Lord. His power, and the wonders He has done."* You don't even have to be a father to obey this Scripture. A man can pass along godly wisdom at any time. Fatherhood is a season where a man can look at his life and intentionally pass along truths to his children. Doing this also builds trust between father and child. The act of mentoring is a powerful relationship tool.

If you are a father of young children, start mentoring them today! Choose a few minutes to talk to them about something important—God's view of work, love, the heart, service, worship, and on and on. If you don't have kids or are beyond those younger years, now is a great time to take someone under your wing and share the wisdom you have with them. I'm in my 50s now, and I crave time with others who are wise beyond my own years. I can't undo mistakes I've made, but I can invest time to keep others from making new ones. That time in the car when your kids just want to play their tunes loud? It's great mentoring time. Strike up a conversation instead. Find out what's going on in their lives and pour in a word of two of wisdom. You don't have to force it. Just be aware of the opportunity and take advantage of it.

Fatherhood is front-loaded

Men, invest time in your children from birth. Make them a priority for your day as long as they are in your house. The time from baby to graduating from high school is the majority of the time you'll have to influence them in life as their father. According to Pew Research, more than 90% of the total time you will spend with your children in their entire life is before the age of 18. Once they become adults, they may see you often—even a few times a week—and talk on the phone. But all of that added together for the remainder of their life will equal about 10% of the total time they'll have with you as their dad.[31]

KIDS TEST US WHEN THEIR LITTLE, AND THEN REJECT US WHEN THEY'RE TEENS, SO WE WAIT IT OUT. BUT THAT'S THE WRONG APPROACH, BECAUSE WE'RE LOSING THE TIME WHEN WE HAVE THE MOST INFLUENCE ON THEIR LIVES.

Fatherhood is front-loaded. We tend to think when our kids are young and we are coming into our own in career or leadership that we'll have plenty of time with them, and we'll most enjoy the moments when they are older. We think we can have more influence on them once they grow up to respect us as adults. When they're small they have their school buddies to play with and aren't interested in us anyway. Kids test us when their little, and then reject us when they're teens, so we wait it out.

But that's the wrong approach, because *we're losing the time when we have the most influence on their lives.* Our greatest opportunity to father them through Scripture, by example and in prayer, is when they are young and living at home. I think of manhood in general as prioritizing a "walk with God" through all facets of life and work. But I think specifically of fatherhood as a man's greatest exercise in time management. A man who walks with God knows *Who* is important. A father must learn *what* is important—what in his life demands his time. *You cannot delegate fatherhood* to someone else.

The moment you think as a father, "I want to spend more time with my children," it's already too late. And you will have that thought. Every father does, just some earlier in the lives of their kids than others. It's too late to recover time that you lost, opportunities to be with them and influence them and love them where you prioritized other things in life and work. But it's never too late to create moments together. When your kids are toddlers, they long to be with you, all the time. You don't have to beg for attention, just enter the same room and engage them. As they get older you have to start working for that time. When they're teenagers, you have to plan it out, tailor your time to their interests. When they're adults, now you're competing with their schedules and priorities. You don't want to humble yourself and ask them, "Would you please spend some time with me?" because you changed their poopy diapers and fed them and paid for their very existence for 25 years and they should be grateful, right?

Will you play with me?
When my oldest daughter—now 19—was about five years old, she loved to play "grocery store". She had a collection of empty food boxes that she would arrange on a shelf, and then set up her toy cash register and grocery cart. She'd come up to my office desk at home and ask, "Dad, will you play with me?" Sometimes I did, but more often than not, I would say, "Sweetie, daddy's working. Maybe in a little while." I recall those days with great guilt now when I see her walk out the door to go spend time with her boyfriend. Occasionally I'll say, "Honey, would you come and talk to me?" Sometimes she does, but more often than not, she'll say, "Dad, I have plans." I don't get upset with her, I get upset with me.

I'm getting the results of the lack of investment I made in the past. Now I have to work for the moments I could have had for free just 15 years ago. This is the great demand of fatherhood—putting aside your life and priorities for time with your children. Do it early and often, because that's when you'll have the most time with them, and the most influence on them, and be the greatest example to them. They'll pick up what you prioritize, whether you like it or not. Jesus said, *"Let the little children come to me, and do not hinder them, for the Kingdom of God belongs to such as these" (Matt 19:14).* Christ had an open-door, open-arms policy for children. So should every father.

Later on
Fatherhood doesn't end when your kids leave the nest. It just gets considerably more expensive. I miss the days when my children would ask for Legos or candy for Christmas. Now they ask for smartphones or concert tickets. Or new tires for their car. In recent years they've taken to just wanting cash. But you'll always be dad, and there will be times when your older children will want your input or advice. Fatherhood moves from provider for the baby to authority for the toddler to pariah for the teenager. Then there's a time when, if you've not done too badly as a dad and maintained a good relationship, you can find yourself an influencer in their life.

My college-age daughter is starting to make some bigger decisions. She's excited about her first real job. I enjoy hearing what is going on in her mind as she shares her day, and her classwork, and what she wants to do in five years. The "later on" is that last 10%—you have already blown through 90% of your time with your kids when they become adults. Cherish that last 10%. As a father, give your full and undivided attention and be for your children's success in life and faith. You can still give a nudge here and there. Never stop speaking the things of God to them, no matter how old they are. And pray for them constantly.

The walk of fatherhood:

- *Have you prayed for your children today?*

- *What does your schedule and commitments for today teach others about the priority of your children and family?*

- *Have you shared any Scripture with your children recently?*

- *What kind of example are you setting for your children with your home and work life?*

- *Are you intentionally taking time to mentor your kids (or others)—giving them your life experience and knowledge so they too can grow in wisdom?*

A MAN SERVES

*"Go forth on your path,
as it exists only
through your walking."*
—St. Augustine of Hippo

Today he is known famously as John Ross, though no one is sure who gave him the moniker. His real name was Charles Rawden Maclean, a boy from Scotland who, at age 13, set out with an expedition of former Royal Naval officers looking for ivory. It was 1825 and he was apprenticed to serve on the 150-ton brig The Mary. The journey took an abrupt turn when they shipwrecked near the coast of southeast Africa.[32]

John Ross was among the first European men to come face to face with the Zulu tribesmen, and their fearsome King Shaka Zulu. The king took Ross and detained him at kwaBulawayo, his stronghold. There he lived for the next few years at the pleasure of the King, serving him and translating for him.[33] A relationship developed, and John Ross soon earned the trust and admiration of Shaka Zulu. The king gave the shipwrecked men permission to stay in his land. They took several years to rebuild the hull in order to put the Mary back under sail.

Two years into their sojourn, the temporary settlement had run of out of medicine and supplies. John Ross, now a young man of just 15, begged King Shaka Zulu to allow him to attempt to walk across Africa and retrieve the supplies from Delagoa Bay. It would be a treacherous journey east to the Indian Ocean. Zulu was impressed by the boy's courage and tenacity, and gave him an escort of ten of his fiercest warriors.

John Ross walked on foot the nearly 400-mile trek to the Portuguese settlement at Delagoa Bay. He traversed uncharted wetlands and mangrove swamps, crocodile- and hippopotamus-infested rivers, and crossed the 1,000-foot wide Tugela River. Ross arrived at his destination and got the needed medicines and supplies, but was appalled by the cruel slave trade he witnessed there. He turned and walked back, taking over three weeks for the journey. Shaka Zulu's warrior escort spread the word of the brave young traveler. John Ross's walk across dark and foreboding Africa quickly became legend.

A year later, with their ship repaired, the crew along with Ross made the return voyage to Scotland. King Shaka Zulu, impressed with the young John Ross, sent emissaries to meet with King George. Ross grew up to captain ships of his own, and to battle against the slave trade. In one incident in Wilmington, North Carolina in 1846, he refused to surrender his black crew members to harbor authorities. He began writing of his convictions in various magazines, including his insights into Zulu culture and his account of the long walk to Delagoa Bay. In his service to King Shaka Zulu, and his 400-mile walk for medicine and supplies, John Ross had become a cultural bridge between the Zulus of South Africa and the Scots.

Ross would continue to influence his homeland away from the slave trade. He died at sea in 1880 and was buried in a pauper's grave. In 2009, the grave was rededicated and a headstone erected. The grave was draped with the new flag of South Africa, and the headstone with the Scottish saltire. John Ross is now known as a true servant of the African and the Scottish people. He embodied the idea of a *servant leader*. He rose to prominence not because he had a great vision or had great authority. He gained respect and influence over others because of the way in which he served them.

Men, serving and leadership
Often men want to develop themselves as leaders. I work for a nonprofit where we mentor men each week in areas of life and leadership. Interestingly, though, this drive to leadership in the Bible is *inferred*. The word "leadership" doesn't appear in the Scriptures. The word "leader" does, but just a few times. There are words in the Testaments like *king, ruler, prince, elder, overseer, pastor, shepherd, elder, bishop,* that certainly allude to leadership.

The word *servant*, however, is mentioned more than 900 times. You'd think in today's world with all of the leadership seminars, workbooks, podcasts, mentoring groups, coaches

YOU CAN HAVE THE LOWEST SCORE ON THE GOLF COURSE, OR BE THE TOP SALESPERSON IN THE OFFICE, OR BE FIRST CHAIR IN THE ORCHESTRA. THAT ISN'T LEADERSHIP. THAT IS JUST BEING IN THE LEAD.

and phone apps that we could look to the Scriptures for more teaching about leadership. The Bible is not chiefly concerned with teaching men how to be leaders. You'll find some leading principles in its pages, but it's not the main point of the book. Instead, the Bible gives great instruction to servants—in ancient culture those of the lowest position. In Bible times only slaves were lower than servants—slaves were owned, servants were paid, but they did many of the same tasks. When Jesus instructed His disciples, *"Anyone who wants to be first must be the very last, and the servant of all" (Mark 9:35)*, He was setting a radical and unexpected tone.

He was equating manhood's highest aim with the lowest role. To His disciples He taught, *If you want to be first, in the best position, in the lead role, then you need to go to the end of the line. Seek instead to serve others.* Servanthood is a set of behaviors and practices that seeks to genuinely better the lives of the people around you. Servanthood encourages a man to foster concern for the needs of others, helping them to reach their highest potential. And this is a core of leadership.

You can have the lowest score on the golf course, or be the top salesperson in the office, or be first chair in the orchestra. This isn't leadership. This is just being *in the lead*. Leadership is always about people, your relationship with them and your influence on their lives. In His conversation with His disciples, Jesus was talking to men who wanted to be first. Instead, He connected serving others to leadership. *You want to be first, disciples? Okay, then be last.* Only through service, helping to better another's life, can you begin to grow closer to them in a way that allows you to lead. When people know you care about them, they'll listen to you and follow you.

Flipping the script

Remember, Jesus had a way of turning religious leaders' philosophies upside down with just a few words. It was among the aspects of His life on earth that drove the leadership of the time—particularly the Jewish community—to detest Him. Long before Jesus walked the earth, the Children of Israel demanded their leader be a king. God gave them what they asked for, and most of those kings were very bad. Through hundreds of years of kings and prophets, Israel waited for the coming King—the promised Messiah. But because they had experience with a monarch for a leader, their view of what Jesus would be like was highly skewed.

They envisioned a conquering king who would vanquish the enemies of Israel and take his rightful place as ruler. But He would be a good and gracious ruler who would treat Israel as she deserved to be treated as the chosen people of God. This king would elevate Israel to greatness. Yes, they would worship this king because He would be the king they had envisioned for their nation.

This is a modern view of leadership. A man may focus on amassing control, so that he might grow in influence by authority. The goal of cultural leadership is to have the most. Control leads to security, and wealth leads to self-sufficiency. A leader is king. The people around him he views as his subjects. Because his has all he needs, he answers to no one.

All of his leadership decisions are in his own best interest. History is filled with these men, who had power, position and possessions, then lost it all. Have you heard of Allen Stanford, Eike Batista, Sean Quinn, Björgólfur Gudmundsson, Aubrey McClendon, Vijay Mallya, Adolf Merckle, or Bill Hwang? They were all influential billionaire leaders of the last 50 years. All died penniless and powerless.

What about Bernie Madoff? Brilliant investor, a founder NASDAQ, influential leader, philanthropist. His riches turned out to be a $17.5 billion Ponzi scheme. He had a reputation as a leader whose smart investments gave financial security to millions of retirees. He was a king on Wall Street. He died of kidney failure while serving a 150-year prison sentence for his crimes. Madoff wanted to be first, in the lead, all for himself. He ended broke, hated, inconsequential, forgotten.

The servant leader
When Jesus arrived by birth in humble surroundings, He hardly seemed destined to be the mighty king that Israel was expecting. Later as Jesus began teaching people, His words about leadership and leading were all the more shocking. His instructions were at odds with influencers of the time. This Man claiming to be the Messiah, the long-awaited King and Conqueror, said: *"The Son of Man did not come to be served, but to serve, and to give his life as a ransom for many"* (Matthew 20:28). Later, Jesus equated Himself to those of greatest need in the world. *"For I was hungry, and you gave me something to eat, I was thirsty, and you gave me something to drink, I was a stranger, and you invited me in, I needed clothes, and you clothed*

me, I was sick, and you looked after me, I was in prison, and you came to visit me" (Matthew 25:35-36).

Surely if you had been a religious authority of the time, the "What the!?" on your face would have been evident. Jesus, in coming from heaven to give His life as a living sacrifice for the sins of all, was a *servant leader.* This is the kind of leadership He was teaching to those who would follow Him. The Apostle Paul reiterated Jesus' teaching in his letter to the Church at Phillippi, *"Do nothing out of selfish ambition or vain conceit. Rather, in humility value others above yourselves, not looking to your own interests but each of you to the interests of the others"* (Philippians 2:3-4).

The Bible teaches that servanthood is man's better pursuit. It will not result in billionaire status or kingly position. But serving others will result in a man being elevated to a role of spiritual and personal influence and impact in the lives of those around him. What are some practical ways that a man can live and model Jesus' brand of servant leadership?

Be present
If leadership is about serving others, it follows you cannot lead outside of the presence of others. Servant leadership cannot be effectively practiced from behind a desk in a closed-door office. You cannot serve your family from the comfort of your recliner. Rather, a servant leader must be among those he is serving. Servant leadership is not accomplished through edict or communiques. Servant leadership is about actions. Jesus tells us in Matthew 5:16, *"In the same way, let your light*

INSTEAD OF MAKING POINTS OR MAKING STATEMENTS, A SERVANT LEADER SEEKS TO HEAR WHAT OTHERS ARE SAYING. LISTEN TO UNDERSTAND INSTEAD OF LISTENING TO RESPOND.

shine before others, that they may see your good deeds and glorify your Father in heaven."

A man serves in the present as he looks for good deeds to engage in throughout his day. Remember that a man is to work. He is created for a purpose. Could it be that your work, your deeds through the day, can accomplish God-honoring service to others? Remember Ephesians 2:10, *"For we are God's handiwork, created in Christ Jesus to do good works, which God prepared in advance for us to do."* When you seek to serve, you will quickly discover the good works God has laid out for you. You will have no lack of influence as a man because there will be no lack of opportunity for you to serve people around you.

Being present also means listening. Instead of making points or making statements, a servant leader hears what others are saying. This gives insight into what they value. In the corporate world we sometimes refer to this as *active listening*—that is, listening to understand versus listening to respond. In this way, a servant leader can more effectively connect to the needs of those around him and influence them toward their best work and effort. Being present in their lives and work builds trust, as they understand you have their best interest at heart. James 1:19 tells men, *"Know this, my beloved brothers: let every person be quick to hear, slow to speak..."*

Be positive
Servant leadership does not come down on people. Rather, it lifts them up through active encouragement. An authoritarian

leader might get things done by voicing the negative consequences of non-compliance. But a servant leader empowers others by sharing the positive benefits that result from their efforts. 1 Thessalonians 5:11 instructs leaders, *"Therefore encourage one another and build each other up, just as in fact you are doing."* This is actually one of my very favorite versus in all the Bible.

One practical way for a man to be positive is to be patient. Here is another area where I am personally challenged. I'm generally a friendly person, but I have a mean streak that comes out when I lose my patience. I know better, though, than to pray for patience, because that just means God is going to give me opportunities to be patient, which means I'll actually have to wait longer and more often. Ephesians 4:2 tells men to interact *"with all humility and gentleness, with patience, bearing with one another in love..."* This idea of "bearing with one another" is to put up with the faults and aspects of character that one just doesn't like about another person. That guy is a jerk. Okay, Jesus says, love him anyway.

Recently I've made it a point to change my attitude in the drive through lane. Fast food restaurants are often—challenged, may be the word—with attracting and retaining sharp, high capacity, engaged employees. Often, I can't understand what they're saying to me at the speaker. It comes out, "WelcometoMcdonaldswillyoubeusingourmobileapptoday?" Then I repeat the order three times. Then they still get it wrong. The person handing me the food has an expression

TO BE HUMBLE IS AN ACTIVE WORK OF THE MIND, PRACTICING MODESTY AND AN ATTITUDE THAT FOCUSES ON RELATIONSHIPS AND REWARDS BEYOND SELF-INTEREST.

that makes me believe their dog just died. Oh, and that meal that was $7.50 a few years ago just cost me $18.

This is a perfect place for me to practice humility, gentleness and patience. Now I always begin with, "Hello, how are you today?" into the speaker. There's usually a pause while they process that someone said something nice to them. "I'm doing okay," comes the reply. "Great, I'm glad to hear it," I'll say, followed by my order. Then at the window a smile and a loud "Thank you so much! I appreciate you." If they seem particularly exasperated by their shift, I might even though in a, "Hang in there, the day will get better I promise!"

I am under no illusion that my kindness at the drive through window is going to result in any kind of butterfly-effect culture shift toward a more positive and supportive society. For me this is just a way to live out 1 Thessalonians 5:11 in a practical sense, and to slowly bleed away the impatience and negativism that has permeated my life for many years. One way a man can serve others is to just be a positive influence in their life, even if it is no more than adding a kind word while ordering a hamburger.

So much of leadership culture is looking for fault or weakness in individuals. A positive leader serves his reports by looking for their best, and raising up their outlook through reinforcing what they are doing well and doing right. The positive leader gets the best from others through focus on encouraging and appreciation. This is a garment that all men can wear. Colossians 3:12 says, *"Put on then, as God's chosen ones,* holy and beloved, compassionate hearts, kindness, humility, meekness, and patience..."

Be last

Leadership teacher Simon Sinek's book, *Leaders Eat Last*, contains simple and effective instruction on servant leadership. He writes, "The true price of leadership is the willingness to place the needs of others above your own. Great leaders truly care about those they are privileged to lead and understand that the true cost of the leadership privilege comes at the expense of self-interest." This is a modern re-telling of Jesus' leadership instructions to His disciples. In Matthew 20:16, Jesus teaches, *"So the last will be first, and the first will be last."*

Sinek argues that a servant leader shows his attitude in simple acts, like waiting to go last in line. The result of this attitude, Sinek writes: "And when a leader embraces their responsibility to care for people instead of caring for numbers, then people will follow, solve problems and see to it that the leader's vision comes to life the right way, a stable way and not the expedient way." Another way to frame this is that men should be humble, not drawing attention to themselves but seeking to serve others with grace and gratitude.

Serving produces humility

One of the greatest benefits of serving others is that it reduces a man's pride and grows his humility. C.S. Lewis said, "A proud man is always looking down on things and people; and, of course, as long as you are looking down, you cannot see something that is above you." At its heart, pride concerns our position. If you approach life and leadership from the position that you have arrived, that you deserve success, and that nobody can tell you how to act or what to do better than you, then your pride will keep you from achieving the very thing you really desire. And it may just destroy you or something you love in the process.

Instead of looking down at everyone and everything, look up. Embrace humility toward others. Express gratitude for what you have. And extinguish the jealousy for what you don't have. Now you will discover your mind is open to others' ideas and directions. Your sense of position will include a sense that your peers' success is also important. And your sense of self-worth will include a healthy concern for the well-being of those around you.

The great danger of pride
Cambyses II was ruler of ancient Persia from 529-522 BC. You have likely never heard of him, but he is famous because in history for one characteristic. During his reign he invaded Egypt and declared himself Pharaoh. He was a ruthless, angry and arrogant man. From the throne of Egypt he then set his sights on invading Ethiopia and sent spies into the land to discover their weaknesses.

The spies brought gifts to the Ethiopian king, and struck up a conversation about trade, but the king was not fooled by their ploy. Instead, the king presented them with a huge bow and told them that the Persians should attack when they

ULTIMATELY LEADERSHIP IS ABOUT THE PEOPLE WE LEAD AND INFLUENCE, AND TO LEAD THEM IS TO SERVE THEM BY ENCOURAGING THEM AND EQUIPPING THEM TO BECOME THEIR VERY BEST.

could muster enough strength to draw the bow as powerfully as he could. Until then they should stay away and thank the gods that their lives were spared. The Ethiopian king was not intimidated. As a final dig at the Persians, the king mentioned that their leader Cambyses would live longer if he stopped eating so badly. Word had gotten to Ethiopia that he was pudgy. The spies went back and reported on the confidence of the Ethiopians.

Cambyses II was incensed by the insults. His pride took over. He immediately sent an invasion force of 50,000 men to attack Ethiopia and reduce the conquered people to slavery, without so much as preparing provisions for the campaign. The soldiers rushed across Africa, and ran out of food long before they arrived in Ethiopia. In desperation, they ate their beasts of burden, and then fed on grass in the fields. When Cambyses II heard of this, the prideful king did not recall his army, but ordered them to advance. The men, having reached the desert sands, cast lots. Thus one man in ten was selected, and the Persian soldiers, with no food or supplies to survive on, began killing and eating each other.

Eventually the army retreated back to Egypt, all nearly dead. They were beaten not by the powerful Ethiopians, but by the pride of their own king, Cambyses II. He was a pathological narcissist who would let his own men result to cannibalism before he would admit that he was wrong. Pride in the traditional sense, going back to the Bible, isn't a positive for men. Pride is associated with conceit, arrogance, self-centeredness and filled with strife. Pride is the deadly sin of superiority—the idea that we can pursue our own self-importance at the expense of others. Cambyses II of Persia is far from the only example of the sin of pride. But he does reveal the great danger of pride, which is that it can blind us to our own mistakes and selfish leadership.

To be humble is an active work of the mind, practicing modesty and an attitude that focuses on relationships and rewards beyond self-interest. Positive leadership is often embodied in the servanthood of a man, one who is "in the trenches" and with his people instead of hovering above them. Here again Christ gives an example saying, *"For who is the greater, one who reclines at the table or one who serves? Is it not the one who reclines at table? But I am among you as the one who serves" (Luke 22:27).* The positive leader views his reports as people he can support through his actions versus a team simply designed to follow his instructions.

The un-leader
Jesus' embrace and teaching of servant leadership was as un-leader a teaching as those in His age had ever heard. As God's chosen people, they had longed for a headstrong, authoritarian leader who would defeat their adversaries and raise them up as first in the world. But that would have only created generations of arrogant, selfish people living under the banner of "Jesus is King!" Instead, Jesus would set a powerful example in His service to us on the cross. Paul writes of Jesus' example: *"Let this mind be in you which was also in Christ Jesus, who, being in the form of God, did not consider it robbery to be equal with God, but made Himself of*

no reputation, taking the form of a bondservant, and coming in the likeness of men. And being found in appearance as a man, He humbled Himself and became obedient to the point of death, even the death of the cross" (Philippians 2:5-8). He showed this attitude time and again in ministry—feeding the people, washing His disciples' feet. Then He went out and lived servant leadership through His death.

A servant leader must unlearn leadership principles that put passion, vision, decisions and administration ahead of people. Ultimately leadership is about the people we lead and influence. To *lead* them is to *serve* them by encouraging them and equipping them to become their very best. To serve them is to meet their basic needs. Consider these simple acts of service in your daily routine:

- Serve someone by helping their family (Romans 12:10).
- Serve someone by donating items they can practically use (Matthew 25:46).
- Serve someone by writing them a note of encouragement (1 Thessalonians 5:11).
- Serve someone by listening to them (James 1:19).
- Serve someone by sharing a meal with them (Acts 20:35).
- Serve someone by doing something good for them even when it is sacrificial or hard (Galatians 6:9).
- Serve someone by sharing an opportunity or blessing you have been given with someone else (Hebrews 13:16).
- Serve someone by thanking them and acknowledging their accomplishment or success (Philippians 2:3).
- Serve someone by paying for something they need, no strings attached (Proverbs 11:24-25).

Servanthood opens the door to deeper and more meaningful and influential relationships. Leadership development, then, is not a race to the top of the ladder, but to be the man that holds the bottom rung, creating a stable platform on which others can rise. In unwinding from traditional leadership, you may instead become the un-leader that really makes a difference.

The walk of service:

- What are some talents, giftedness and abilities you have that could be used in service to others?

- In what circles are you an influence? How might service to that group of people (family, coworkers, industry professionals, customers, friends) establish your ability to lead them toward Christ?

- How can you be of service to the people closest to you today (your wife, your children, your immediate work circle, your church)

A MAN WALKS

"The sum of the whole is this: to walk and be happy; to walk and be healthy. The best way to lengthen out our days is to walk steadily and with purpose."
—Charles Dickens

Every July in the Netherlands, tens of thousands of people descend on the city of Nijmegen. They're participating in the Walk of the World, also called the *Vierdaagse of Nijmegen*. (I'm going to use the "Walk of the World" from this point, because, no offense meant to the Dutch, but I can't pronounce that many vowels in a row.) The annual event consists of walking—quite a bit of walking. Participants walk 30 to 50 kilometers (between 19 and 31 miles) a day for four days.[34] It's a walk filled with people of all ages and backgrounds.

Why do it? For the exercise, of course. The walk itself is through the beautiful Dutch countryside. And there are scores of interesting characters, which makes for great people-watching. The Walk of the World began as a military exercise in 1909. They canceled it a few times—like after Germany invaded in 1940, and again during the 2020 pandemic. About 40,000 take part in this now mostly-civilian event. In 2016 the Walk of the World celebrated it's One Hundredth Anniversary. Along with the walk are all kinds of concerts, exhibits, fireworks and other festivities known as the *Vierdaagsefeesten*, attended by over a million people.[35]

On the closing day of the event, usually a Friday, participants near the finish. Fans along the route present the walkers with gladioli, a beautiful flower that has been a symbol of victory for centuries. In ancient Rome they showered gladiators with these flowers. They call the last stretch the Via Gladiola. People bring their lawn chairs and watch the walkers pass by. Dutch TV broadcasts the finish.

It takes tremendous endurance to walk 50 kilometers a day for a week. Many participants don't finish. In 2006, two participants died, and others required medical attention, because of extreme heat. The secret to The Walk of the World is not great strength, but rather great stamina. It's a marathon of sorts, and those who finish the Walk must come prepared, physically and mentally. Some participate in the Walk every year. The record is held by Bert van der Lans, who completed his seventy-first Walk in 2018 at the age of 86. In many ways I think the Walk of the World imitates the walk of life itself, which takes great stamina, and is filled with lots of colorful characters, and can end in great personal victory, and sometimes tremendous tragedy.

Learning to walk

My two daughters are adopted from China, and came to our family at 18 months and 4 years, respectively. They were already walking when we met them at their orphanages. My son, though, we had as a foster child from birth. He arrived at our house straight from the hospital. It was an odd experience that our third child was the only one that we saw as he was learning to walk.

When learning to walk, kids have a specific process. Doctors have every step recorded and written out, and this is one way they can tell if a child is ahead or behind in their physical development. First, a baby needs to learn how to roll over on their stomach. Then they'll push up onto their arms and hands. Next, they'll learn how to pull their body into a vertical position, usually with the support of furniture or mom or dad. Then they may do something called *cruising*, which is squatting or walking while leaning against the wall or other objects for support. Finally, they'll stand unassisted and balance on their legs, before taking those first independent steps. Toddlers typically walk about two months after learning to stand. All of this happens in sequence between 9 to 16 months of age. By a year and a half old, most kids are walking independently.[36]

I loved watching my son Levi once he started walking. His curiosity increased significantly once he was able to move himself about. He only had one speed at that age, which was "as fast as I can". He wanted to be everywhere, seeing everything, all at once. Before he was walking, he kinda sat and explored himself—looked at his hands, figured out the ways he could bend his legs, rolled around on the carpet.

When he started walking, Levi began taking an interest in the world and people around him. His inward focus turned outward, and his legs took him to any curiosity. When a child learns to walk, I think a subtle shift occurs in the mind. He moves from thinking about himself to thinking about all the facets of his environment, and how he fits in it.

Made to walk
The human body was designed for walking. Not running—which we can do, but not like a cheetah. We weren't made for heavy lifting. Nor for swimming. All of these are possible, but we're adept at walking like no other species in the world. The placement of the hips, the size and stride of the legs. The toes for balance and pushing off in stride. The relatively small upper body and head in terms of weight to be carried. One leg touching the ground at all times. If you're an average man you'll walk 2-3 miles today. Wake up, walk to the bathroom, the shower, the closet, the kitchen. Walk around at work, at lunch. Walk into the store in the evening.

I'm amazed when I see athletes run, jump, throw, catch, slide, with great skill and talent. Physically it's incredible to watch because some of it doesn't seem possible. I have to wonder how much practice, strength and effort it takes to do some of the things they do. Walking, on the other hand, is the simplest, most natural-looking physical activity I might witness. Everyone can do it. Slow and steady, transporting our head

WE WERE MADE
IN GOD'S IMAGE
AND GOD HIMSELF
IS A WALKER.
JUST READ GENESIS 3:8.
AND GOD MADE
MAN TO WALK.

and hands from here to there for this task or that. We were made in God's image and God Himself is a walker. This is absolutely true—*"And they heard God walking in the garden in the cool of the day..." Genesis 3:8.*

God was among the trees. God made noise when He walked. That only happens if legs and feet are in motion, feet touching the ground and leaves. I don't know what God looks like, but if I'm made in His image, certainly He could manifest Himself to Adam and Eve with hands and feet and legs and arms. He is quite capable of taking a pleasant stroll through His creation. Just as God made man in His image and gave him certain capabilities, I believe God made man to walk, and talks about walking, for a reason. The fact we walk to get around wasn't happenstance—after all God made fish to swim and birds to fly. Man walks. Why?

Walking as a godly man
The reality of "walking like a man" as I've written about here is that all of this together is impossible for a man. Can a man really work, love, guard, fear, father and serve? The duties of manhood far outstrip the abilities of man. That is, except in Christ. I believe one of the reasons God describes our relationship with Him as a walk in Scripture is man's tendency to regard his spiritual condition as a portion of his life, versus the central theme of his entire existence. God wants us to understand that being the godly man means adapting a specific and God-given lifestyle. It can be explained as something that we're already made to do and can do well—walking.

God describes our relationship with him through life as a walk. The nature of the action gives us a clue as to God's desire for us. We pick up walking early on in life, we learn to stand on our feet, and then it becomes a natural part of our day, something we don't even think about and something we do well. When we read God's instructions for our lives in Micah 6:8, we should find them comforting: *"And what does the Lord require of you? To act justly and to love mercy and to walk humbly with your God."* Do you want to really please God with your life? Then walk with Him.

A verse with three simple instructions, but rich in content. What does it mean to walk humbly with God? We know how to walk, so that verse must mean, in part, that we have a continuous, ongoing activity associated with God. We're not static when we're walking, we're in motion. A man who walks with God doesn't make a one-time decision to follow God. He doesn't say "yes" to God as a teenager, and then have no evidence of that relationship through life. Walking with God is constant, daily. The Bible speaks frequently about walking. There's a clear sense that a steady, purposeful, intentional walk with God is a duty for which man was created. From beginning to end, God's Word reminds us to walking faithfully with God:

"These are the generations of Noah. Noah was a righteous man, blameless in his generation. Noah walked with God" (Genesis 6:9).

"When Abram was ninety-nine years old the Lord appeared to Abram and said to him, 'I am God Almighty; walk before me, and be blameless...'" (Genesis 17:1).

"And I will walk among you and will be your God, and you shall be my people" (Leviticus 26:12).

"You shall walk in all the ways that the Lord your God has commanded you, that you may live, and that it may go well with you, and that you may live long in the land that you shall possess" (Deuteronomy 5:33).

"You shall teach them diligently to your children, and shall talk of them when you sit in your house, and when you walk by the way, and when you lie down, and when you rise"(Deuteronomy 6:7).

"So you shall keep the commandments of the Lord your God by walking in his ways and by fearing him" (Deuteronomy 8:6).

"'And now, Israel, what does the Lord your God require of you, but to fear the Lord your God, to walk in all his ways, to love him, to serve the Lord your God with all your heart and with all your soul...'" (Deuteronomy 10:12).

"And keep the charge of the Lord your God, walking in His ways and keeping His statutes, His commandments, His rules, and His testimonies... that the Lord may establish His Word that he spoke concerning me, saying, 'If your sons pay close attention to their way, to walk before Me in faithfulness with all their heart and with all their soul, you shall not lack a man on the throne of Israel'" (1 Kings 2:3-4).

"Blessed is the man who walks not in the counsel of the wicked, nor stands in the way of sinners..." (Psalm 1:1).

"Teach me your way, O Lord, that I may walk in your truth; unite my heart to fear your name" (Psalm 86:11).

"Blessed are the people who know the festal shout, who walk, O Lord, in the light of your face..." (Psalm 89:15).

"I will ponder the way that is blameless. Oh when will you come to me? I will walk with integrity of heart within my house..." (Psalm 101:2).

"Blessed are those whose way is blameless, who walk in the law of the Lord!" (Psalm 119:1).

"He stores up sound wisdom for the upright; he is a shield to those who walk in integrity..." (Proverbs 2:7).

"I walk in the way of righteousness, in the paths of justice..." (Proverbs 8:20).

"Whoever walks with the wise becomes wise, but the companion of fools will suffer harm" (Proverbs 13:20).

"The righteous who walks in his integrity— blessed are his children after him!" (Proverbs 20:7).

"When you pass through the waters, I will be with you; and through the rivers, they shall not overwhelm you; when you walk through fire you shall not be burned, and the flame shall not consume you, for I am the Lord your God, the Holy One..." (Isaiah 43:2-3).

SOMETIMES WE HAVE A PICTURE OF GOD WHERE HE IS FAR, FAR AWAY, LIVING IN THE CLOUDS OR IN SPACE OR SOME OTHER FANTASTIC REALM. THAT COULDN'T BE FURTHER FROM THE TRUTH.

"Thus says the Lord: 'Stand by the roads, and look, and ask for the ancient paths, where the good way is; and walk in it, and find rest for your souls.'" (Jeremiah 6:16).

"Again Jesus spoke to them, saying, 'I am the light of the world. Whoever follows me will not walk in darkness, but will have the light of life'" (John 8:12).

"We were buried therefore with him by baptism into death, in order that, just as Christ was raised from the dead by the glory of the Father, we too might walk in newness of life" (Romans 6:4).

"But I say, walk by the Spirit, and you will not gratify the desires of the flesh" (Galatians 5:16).

"If we live by the Spirit, let us also walk in step with the Spirit" (Galatians 5:25).

"I therefore, a prisoner for the Lord, urge you to walk in a manner worthy of the calling to which you have been called..." (Ephesians 4:1).

"And walk in love, as Christ loved us and gave himself up for us, a fragrant offering and sacrifice to God" (Ephesians 5:2).

"For at one time you were darkness, but now you are light in the Lord. Walk as children of light" (Ephesians 5:8).

"Look carefully then how you walk, not as unwise but as wise..." (Ephesians 5:15).

"So as to walk in a manner worthy of the Lord, fully pleasing to him: bearing fruit in every good work and increasing in the knowledge of God..." (Colossians 1:10).

"Therefore, as you received Christ Jesus the Lord, so walk in him..." (Colossians 2:6).

"Walk in wisdom toward outsiders, making the best use of the time. Let your speech always be gracious, seasoned with salt, so that you may know how you ought to answer each person." Colossians 4:5-6

"Finally, then, brothers, we ask and urge you in the Lord Jesus, that as you received from us how you ought to walk and to please God, just as you are doing, that you do so more and more" (1 Thessalonians 4:1).

"Whoever says he abides in Him ought to walk in the same way in which He walked" (1 John 2:6).

"And this is love, that we walk according to his commandments; this is the commandment, just as you have heard from the beginning, so that you should walk in it" (2 John 1:6).

All of these Scriptures point to a relationship between man and God where man is close to God, obedient, attentive, humble. Sometimes we have a picture of God where He is "in a galaxy far, far away," living in the clouds or in space or some other fantastic realm. We're down here on earth. We phone Him up in prayer from time to time, and are left with this book of instructions called the Bible, but otherwise it's a long distance relationship. That couldn't be further from the truth. Consider six ways we can walk with God daily:

A man can walk in harmony

Walking with God signifies that one is listening to God and His commands, is obedient, has placed his faith in God, and is following along God's path for his life. In this we experience the greatest benefit of walking with God—a deep relationship with Him. As we daily seek God and communicate with Him through prayer and His Word, we experience all that following along His path has to offer. Psalm 15:11 teaches, *"You make known to me the path of life; you will fill me with joy in your presence, with eternal pleasures at your right hand."* When we obey God's Word and have our faith in God, the Bible describes this walk as pleasurable and joyful. We don't have to walk in fear of God, but in Christ we are His friends (John 15:14, 1 John 4:12-14).

A man can walk with confidence

The Bible indicates that walking with God gives us comfort and confidence. In Psalm 23:4, King David says, *"Though I walk through the valley of the shadow of death, I will fear no evil, for you are with me."* This Psalm highlights God's protection and presence for those who walk with Him. Even in our dark and challenging situations we can be assured that God is there with us. In fact, God *"guides [us] along the right paths for His Name's sake"* (Psalm 23:3). We build confidence in God when we consistently rely on Him for help in every situation. The result is a growing faith, knowing that as we walk with God, we are guided by Him along the path of life.

A man can walk with stamina

God grants us the vitality and stamina to walk with Him, even in hard choices and difficult situations. Isaiah 40:31 promises, *"...those who hope in the Lord will renew their strength. They will soar on wings like eagles; they will run and not grow weary, they will walk and not be faint."* Walking with God will not be easy. Have you even gotten tired from life? The challenging conversations, the tough daily choices, trying to connect to difficult people, managing the many priorities of marriage, home, the workplace—and do it all in a godly way with patience and humility and perseverance—it is exhausting! The Bible promises that those who walk with God will receive the energy to sustain our physical and mental effort.

A man can walk with trust

When we walk with God, He will grant us a path that is trustworthy. Proverbs 3:5-6 reminds us to *"Trust in the Lord with all your heart and lean not on your own understanding; in all your ways submit to him, and he will make your paths straight."* A curving path has surprises around the turns, but God's straight path is true and trustworthy. Trusting God means we live believing in His reliability, the truth of His Word, and His abilities. This is more than "feeling good" about God, it's a choice to believe that what He has said is true. The Bible teaches that best course to get to God's desired destination is to trust Him and walk in His ways.

A man can walk in light

We need to be able to see where we are going. Light keeps us from stumbling around in the dark. 1 John 1:7 promises, *"But if we walk in the light, as he is in the light, we have fellowship one with another, and the blood of Jesus Christ his Son cleanses us from all sin."* Walking in the light is to be transparent, in full view of others, where they can see our faith in Christ. Paul said he was sent *"to open their eyes so that they may turn from darkness to light and from the dominion of Satan to God."* The Gospel message calls sinners to turn to Christ *"out of darkness into His marvelous light" (1 Peter 2:9).* Jesus Himself is the light Who lights our way (John 1:4, John 14:6). Living in sin we want to hide and walk in the shadows, but in Christ we can walk in the light (which is His light).

A man can walk in truth
3 John 3 recounts, *"For I was very glad when brethren came and testified to your truth, that is, how you are walking in truth."* John is saying that it is not enough just to hold the truth—whether it's the Bible in hand or a doctrine in our mind—but we can walk as people who live out these truths.

Look at the truths in Philippians 3:3-8: *"Do nothing out of selfish ambition or vain conceit. Rather, in humility value others above yourselves, not looking to your own interests but each of you to the interests of the others. In your relationships with one another, have the same mindset as Christ Jesus: Who, being in very nature God, did not consider equality with God something to be used to his own advantage; rather, he made himself nothing by taking the very nature of a servant, being made in human likeness. And being found in appearance as a man, he humbled himself by becoming obedient to death— even death on a cross!"* God's Word is filled with practical instruction on how to walk daily with Him through our words, attitudes and actions—this is but one example.

"Abide, abide, abide, I'm right here by your side."
1 John 2:6 describes our connection to God as *"abiding in Him"*. The true picture of God is that He is with us at all times, as we walk through life and work and home and family and tragedy and triumph. We don't walk *to* God, like we are working our way to heaven. We walk *with* God, as man first did in the Garden. The walk of man is to *abide* with God continually.

Our family dog is a chocolate Labrador retriever named Georgia. She loves to jump and run, to take walks outdoors and to play tug of war with any object in the house she is not supposed to have. Georgia spends most of her time laying down, snuggling, napping. My office in the house is downstairs near the front door. When I start working in the morning, Georgia comes downstairs to a certain chair she has claimed as her own and stays near me. She makes a soft groan when she lays down to announce her presence, and desire for a dog treat and for me to rub her ears.

When my daughter Zoey gets home from school, Georgia moves up to her bedroom, where she parks herself on the floor as Zoey does her homework. Then Keri my wife gets home from teaching and Georgia moves to the kitchen, where she relaxes by the refrigerator while dinner is in progress. After dinner we move to the living room, and so does Georgia. Then at bedtime, Georgia moves up and jumps on the foot of my bed where I might read or watch TV before going to sleep.

Georgia is an abiding dog. She just wants to be wherever we are. If we empty out of a room and move to another area of the house, so does Georgia. Are you a man who abides with God? Do you just want to be wherever God is? Do you have a sense as you walk through your day that God is by your side? As you go through projects and meetings and errands and presentations and appointments, do you constantly think about God's presence and how He would want you to handle the moment?

Our dog Georgia has a voice. Years ago my wife and I started talking in "dog voice". We often have conversations through the dog. I know it sounds odd, but it's just a family quirk and it's fun for us. "Hi mom, I had a great day today and I'm wagging my tail for you!" I will say in my Georgia voice. "Dad, myself needs to go outside when you get a chance," Keri says in her Georgia voice. The kids heard this from their earliest years and now they also speak through the dog as well. Georgia has a cute face and she's a smart dog. We know what she would say if given the chance. So we say it for her.

Once when Keri was studying the concept of abiding in Christ, she realized our dog was an abiding dog. So Georgia said a little line to me through Keri. "Abide, abide, abide, I'm right here by your side." Eventually we turned it into a song. Now whenever we find Georgia abiding with us in the room we'll sing the phrase. "Abide, abide, abide, I'm right here by your side." An abiding man longs to have God at his side all day, in every room where he might go. As he walks through life he has the constant thought that God is there right by his side.

ARE YOU A MAN WHO ABIDES WITH GOD? DO YOU JUST WANT TO BE WHEREVER GOD IS? DO YOU HAVE A SENSE AS YOU WALK THROUGH YOUR DAY THAT GOD IS BY YOUR SIDE?

A walk to eternity

Of all the ordinary people named in the Bible, I think I am most intrigued by Enoch. He's only mentioned across a few verses. We know Enoch was the son of Jared, and that at age 65 he became the father of Methuselah. The Bible also tells us Enoch lived 365 years. He was the great-grandfather of Noah. The book of Jude mentions Enoch as "seventh from Adam", so we know he lived early in creation, before the flood, after the Garden of Eden, when the people of earth had begun to nose-dive into sinful decline.

Then Genesis 5:24 says, *"Enoch walked faithfully with God; then he was no more, because God took him away."* I fascinated by people whose whole life is summed up in one sentence. He walked faithfully with God. So much so, that at some point, as most scholars believe, he just kept walking one day right into heaven. How do we know that Enoch did not die? He is also mentioned in the New Testament. Hebrews 11:5 recounts, *"By faith Enoch was taken up so that he should not see death, and he was not found, because God had taken him. Now before he was taken he was commended as having pleased God."*

Before the days of Google and smart phones and encyclopedias and Ancestry.com, we know of Enoch because he walked with God. That simple, daily act was so profound that Enoch was renowned from Genesis until Hebrews— about 3,500 years of history. Enoch didn't build an ark, or part the sea, or slay a giant, or write the letters of the New Testament. He was just an ordinary guy. But he spent his entire life walking faithfully with God.

That, really, was all God wanted or expected of him. And this pleased God so much that, one day, God let him continue walking. He walked past his house, past the end of the field, past the woods and the pasture, past the hills and mountain. And before he knew it, he had walked to heaven. What an amazing ending to the walk of man! What a wonderful reward for a life that was faithfully walked.

The walk of man:

- *How do you walk daily with God? What is the evidence in your life as a man that you are walking with God?*

- *Do you have a sense of God's presence with you in life and work? What actions and attitudes can you have that help you to abide in God at all times?*

- *Are the steps you are walking today leading you closer to heaven? Like Enoch, is your walk with God growing and faithful?*

WALK LIKE A MAN

I have a t-shirt that reads, "Not all who wander are lost". That's true, but all who wander aren't making progress toward a destination. Walking without God through life is just wandering around. God makes the walk meaningful, because you are headed somewhere with Someone. You cannot walk like a man if that walk is without God. A walk without God is a walk without purpose and intent. It means nothing outside of your own two feet.

I never knew you
It might appear to those who have known me for years that my walk with God began at an early age, but it didn't. My parents were Christians and brought my brother and I to church from an early age. We grew up going to all of the church activities. I told them I wanted to commit my life to Jesus when I was 12 years old. I walked down to the front of the church with them. I was baptized. I kept going to church throughout my teenage years. I participated in Sunday School and youth choir and went to church camp in the summer. The reality, though, is that I kept on living for myself.

I loved technology and graphic arts and during my high school years I worked at a computer store doing installs and training. After high school I took a job at the local church I attended, which grew into a full-time role doing communications and graphic arts for various ministries. I was completely surrounded by good people and good ministries, and excellent Christian teaching. I had fantastic avenues to learn and serve and grow in faith.

But I didn't. I was in God's house all day every day, but I wasn't walking with Him. I knew lots of facts and teachings of Jesus, but I did not have a relationship with Him. I was going through the motions, walking on my own. If you got close enough to me you could see I really wasn't walking with God, because I wasn't spending any time with Him daily. I wasn't praying. I wasn't serving. I wasn't growing. I wasn't submitting anything in my life to God of meaning or merit. It is exceedingly easy in our culture to look like a godly man and not actually be one.

Jesus talks about people like me in Matthew 7:21-23. He said, *"Not everyone who says to Me, 'Lord, Lord,' shall enter the kingdom of heaven, but he who does the will of My Father in heaven. Many will say to Me in that day, 'Lord, Lord, have we not prophesied in Your name, cast out demons in Your name, and done many wonders in Your name?' And then I will declare to them, 'I never knew you; depart from Me, you who practice lawlessness!'"* Scary words, but true of me at that point in my life. He could have also said, "Not everyone who says they walk with Me really does."

I walked on my own well into my 30s. It was at that point that some great men in my life called me to account. Sin had grown in my life, and I had over time betrayed friends and colleagues. I had lied to my wife. In my walk as a man, I had left the road and gone down my own path and now it was thick and thorny and rocky. It was at that point that I surrendered my life to Jesus Christ. In church circles, I used to hear the phrase, "I decided to follow Jesus." I don't believe that's true, because it sounds like a light choice, just an option one picks from the various paths before them. Like buying a car or getting your teeth cleaned. No, this was a *surrender*. I'm giving up on my own walk now, God. You lay out the path now. I'm going to walk with You. I'm no longer in charge.

Nothing and everything changed

Of walking with God I would say two things. First, it is much, much harder. To look at each facet of life and work in light of walking with God is not easy. Honestly, though, we men were warned. In Matthew 16:24, *"Then Jesus said to His disciples, 'Whoever wants to be My disciple must deny themselves and take up their cross and follow Me.'"* Ouch. That's true. To deny yourself is this unselfish, humble, loving, patient manhood the Bible talks about. Walking with God is sacrificial and selfless.

Walking with God means the path is clearly laid out, but sometimes there are people along the side of the road throwing rocks. Here's the reality with God: My kids are still hard to parent. I have difficulty making time for all the responsibilities I have. The car breaks down when there's no extra money in the bank. I have a fantastic day in one area,

TO WALK LIKE A MAN IS ENTIRELY DEPENDENT ON WHO YOU ARE WALKING WITH. THE PERSON YOU CHOOSE TO WALK THROUGH LIFE WITH INDICATES THE KIND OF MAN YOU WANT TO BE AND BECOME.

only to realize I completely missed something important in another. I naïvely thought this walk with God would be liberating and unburdened. Didn't Jesus say, *"For my yoke is easy and my burden is light" (Matthew 11:30)?* Sometimes I get the feeling that nothing has changed.

And yet everything has changed. When you walk on your own, the best you can hope for is to wander well, find your way to some pleasant places along the way, but otherwise have no real destination. When you walk with God, you can truly enjoy the journey. It's possible now to walk like a man. Walking with God I now am beginning to understand:
- I can walk in work that is pleasing to God.
- I can walk in love selflessly and sacrificially, following the example of God.
- I can walk as a guard, keeping my heart pure and strong for God.
- I can walk with a healthy fear of God, treating Him with respect and awe.
- I can walk in fatherhood, being an example of godliness to my children.
- I can walk in service, living humbly and leading others toward God.
- I can walk with God Himself, in a growing relationship, pleasing Him and following Him along the path He has laid out for me.

I have learned to walk like a man is entirely dependent on Who you are walking with. The Person you choose to walk through life with indicates the kind of man you want to be and become. Author and evangelist Leonard Ravenhill said, "Smart men walked on the moon, daring men walked on the ocean floor, but wise men walk with God." That's an interesting perspective. When all is said and done, would I like to be remembered as one who was smart, daring, or wise? Which of this would bring the most value from my life to those around me? It depends entirely on the Person I choose to walk with.

Join God on the walk

If you are not a man walking with God today, I would invite you, urge you—even beg you—to begin that walk with Him now. Save yourself the mistake of walking on your own through life, then finding the finish line does not lead you to heaven. Don't fake the walk like I did, and think that saying "Lord, Lord" on the day of judgment will get you into heaven, not having really chosen to walk with God. Instead, surrender now to God. You can begin immediately. All you have to do is ask, and mean it.

Find your own words, but pray something like, "Dear Jesus, I have been walking on my own all of these years. I have sinned against you and displeased you and I'm wandering in life and work. I'm been following my own path instead of the one You laid out for me. I realize I can't save myself, or work my way to heaven. I'm turning my life over to You right now. You are in charge. Forgive me for disobeying you. Help me to walk with You every day, learning from You and living my life for Your purpose. Make me the man You desire me to be. I pray this in Your Name, Amen."

To begin this walk in earnest, do two things. First, find a local church where you can begin to walk with God in all areas of life, family and work. Make an appointment and talk to your Pastor, telling him about the decision you have made to walk with Jesus. Second, find a group of Christian men you can walk with. The ministry I serve has men meeting at Leadership Tables every week in various locations. Small groups meet to study the Bible and live out its teachings. You can learn more about us and connect with a table—or start your own—at leadershiptable.org.

Knowing versus proving

Since ancient times, men have attempted to walk barefoot through fire. You've seen accounts of those who walk across hot coals without being burned. Firewalking is done as a part of cultures in India, Greece, Spain, China, Japan, Bulgaria, Sri Lanka, Thailand, Fiji, Tibet and other places around the world.[37] Almost always with firewalking there is a religious component, though most organized churches and sects frown on the practice. Participants often enter a period of purification before their attempt for days in advance. They take baths, refuse food, or don't speak for a time. There is no smoking, drinking or sex during the purification time.

Doctors and psychologists have examined firewalkers, and often find their experience genuine. A man will slowly walk across white-hot burning coals and not be burned. Sometimes the presence of hard callouses on the feet, where the firewalker has gone barefoot for years, provides some explanation. The firewalking is often accompanied by crowds

SAVE YOURSELF THE MISTAKE OF WALKING ON YOUR OWN THROUGH LIFE, THEN FINDING THE FINISH LINE DOES NOT LEAD YOU TO HEAVEN. DON'T FAKE THE WALK LIKE I DID.

of onlookers and music. It may be done in honor of a saint, or in memory of a friend, in commemoration of a holiday, or as a rite of passage into a priesthood. Year after year, men take off their shoes and try to walk on fire without getting burned. But why do men volunteer to attempt this dangerous walk?

There are men who know their worth, and those who are trying to prove their worth. To some degree, firewalkers have something to prove, maybe to themselves or maybe to the crowd or their friends or the world. If they're able to make the walk without getting burned, they'll be worthy. They'll be thought of as brave, or faithful, or strong. When it comes to our Almighty God, He doesn't require of His creation, man, to prove anything to Him. We don't have to walk across the burning hot coals. We don't have to walk into a volcano.

God confirmed our worth when He sent His Son to die for us on a cross. He made us, and when we sinned against Him, He gave us a means to resume our walk with our Creator. And He does not require of us grand gestures, feats of strength or shocking sacrifice. No, His requirement for man is simple and straightforward. *"And what does the Lord require of you? To act justly and to love mercy and to walk humbly with your God"* (Micah 6:8).

Come, put your shoes on. Look to the path ahead. Turn to your side and see Christ leading the way. Now, it is your turn to Walk Like a Man.

WHEN IT COMES
TO OUR ALMIGHTY GOD,
HE DOESN'T REQUIRE
OF HIS CREATION, MAN,
TO PROVE ANYTHING
TO HIM. WE DON'T
HAVE TO WALK INTO
A VOLCANO.

ENDNOTES

1. https://www.statista.com/statistics/595249/millennials-live-in-their-parents-home-gender/
2. https://ibhus.com/mental-health/are-lonely-single-men-on-the-rise-and-why
3. https://www.pewresearch.org/short-reads/2014/12/22/less-than-half-of-u-s-kids-today-live-in-a-traditional-family/
4. https://en.wikipedia.org/wiki/Chromosome
5. https://www.businessinsider.com/lgbtq-cartoon-characters-kids-database-2021-06
6. https://en.wikipedia.org/wiki/Chivalry
7. https://fox59.com/news/national-world/teen-who-went-viral-walking-for-work-now-paying-it-forward-with-new-foundation/
8. https://www.cbsnews.com/news/men-workforce-work-companies-struggle-fill-jobs-manufacturing/
9. https://www.milkenreview.org/articles/the-male-non-working-class
10. https://www.zippia.com/advice/career-change-statistics.
11. https://www.linkedin.com/pulse/pros-cons-long-term-employment-same-organization-rocky-cobb/
12. https://www.psychologytoday.com/us/blog/he-speaks-she-speaks/202205/failure-and-burnout-are-tough-on-men
13. https://hbr.org/2006/12/extreme-jobs-the-dangerous-allure-of-the-70-hour-workweek
14. https://en.wikipedia.org/wiki/Hilaire_Belloc
15. https://www.defense.gov/multimedia/experience/tomb-of-the-unknown-soldier/
16. https://www.armyupress.army.mil/Journals/NCO-Journal/Archives/2013/January/Humble-Reverence-Eternal-Vigilance/
17. https://www.dentinstitute.com/22-facts-about-the-brain-world-brain-day/
18. https://www.cnn.com/2022/11/29/health/men-friendships-wellness/index.html
19. https://grandcanyonwest.com/things-to-do/skywalk/
20. https://www.nimh.nih.gov/health/statistics/specific-phobia
21. https://www.nimh.nih.gov/health/statistics/any-anxiety-disorder
22. https://pubmed.ncbi.nlm.nih.gov/32852735/
23. https://www.healthline.com/health/mental-health/fight-flight-freeze
24. https://www.homecareassistancetampabay.com/common-fears-of-the-elderly/
25. https://www.crossway.org/articles/what-does-2-timothy-17-mean/
26. https://biblehub.com/lexicon/exodus/20-20.htm
27. https://jamesriver.church/blog/how-should-we-fear-god
28. https://www.gotquestions.org/jealous-God.html
29. https://americafirstpolicy.com/issues/issue-brief-fatherlessness-and-its-effects-on-american-society
30. https://eric.ed.gov/?id=EJ985577
31. https://www.pewresearch.org/social-trends/2024/01/25/young-adults-relationship-with-their-parents/

32 https://en.wikipedia.org/wiki/Charles_Rawden_Maclean
33 ·https://www.scotsman.com/arts-and-culture/the-legend-of-john-ross-who-became-a-hero-at-12-1488872
34 https://wildernesscoffee-naturalhigh.com/vierdaagse-nijmegen-long-distance-walk-trials-tribulations/
35 https://en.wikipedia.org/wiki/International_Four_Days_Marches_Nijmegen
36 https://blog.lovevery.com/skills-stages/walking/
37 https://www.penn.museum/sites/expedition/the-strange-practice-of-fire-walking/

FOR MORE FREE RESOURCES ON GROWING IN MANHOOD AND LEADERSHIP, VISIT LEADERSHIPTABLE.ORG.

Thank you...
To Keri Mason for the encouragement.
To Eden and Zoey Mason for the kindness.
To Levi Mason for the challenge.
To Chris White Sr. for the wisdom.
To Glen Jackson for the confidence.
To Chad Boles for the edits.
To Dave Dorries for the ideas.
To Dave McWhorter for the counsel.
To Jeff Shaw for the trust.
To Colin White for the example.
To Jim Braun for the support.
To Mark and Renée Maynard for the friendship.
To Charles Reynolds for the prayer.
To Georgia for the snuggles.

Eugene Mason

I welcome the opportunity to talk with you about what it means to Walk Like a Man. Please contact me directly at walklikeaman@leadmin.org. Find more resources on Walking Like a Man at walklikeaman.org.

www.ingramcontent.com/pod-product-compliance
Lightning Source LLC
Chambersburg PA
CBHW070850050426
42453CB00012B/2123